Countdown to THANKSGIVING

Amy Puetz

Memory Making Stories & Activities for 14 Days Leading up to Thanksgiving

Published by
Golden Prairie Press
P.O. Box 429
Wright, WY 82732
307-464-0266

www.AmyPuetz.com

Printed Book ISBN: 978-1-62492-020-2
Ebook ISBN: 978-1-62492-021-9

Copyright 2015 by Amy Puetz
All Rights Reserved.
No part of this book may be reproduced in any form or by any electronic or mechanical means including information storage and retrieval systems, without permission in writing from the author. The only exception is by a reviewer, who may quote short excerpts in a review.

Cover & Layout Design by Amy Puetz

Images from the Library of Congress, out of print books, and Amy Puetz.

Contents

Introduction..1

14 Days Until Thanksgiving..3
    First Harvest-Home in Plymouth by W. DeLoss Love, Jr. 4, The First Thanksgiving 5, Harvest Hunt 6, Countdown to Thanksgiving printable calendar 6

13 Days Until Thanksgiving..7
    How Obadiah Brought About Thanksgiving by Emily Hewitt Leland 8, "We Thank Thee," by Ralph Waldo Emerson 13, Thanksgiving Song—"Count Your Blessings" 14

12 Days Until Thanksgiving..15
    The Soap Making of Remember Biddle by Carolyn Sherwin Bailey 16, Thanksgiving Quiz 19

11 Days Until Thanksgiving..20
    Davy's Thanksgiving by J. T. Trowbridge 21, Thanksgiving Before the Pilgrims 25, Thanksgiving Song—"Harvest Hymn" 26

10 Days Until Thanksgiving..27
    Captain Christy's Thanksgiving by Carolyn Sherwin Bailey 28, "Poem for Thanksgiving" by Isaac Watts, Pilgrim Collar and Bonnet 31

9 Days Until Thanksgiving..32
    The Story of Massasoit by Robert Mackenzie 33, "Thanksgiving" by F. R. Havergal 34, National Monument to the Forefathers 35, Hat and Indian Headdress 36

8 Days Until Thanksgiving..37
    The Mother of Thanksgiving by Amy Puetz 38, Excerpt from *Godey's Lady's Book Magazine* by Sarah Josepha Hale 39, Our National Thanksgiving Day by Sarah Hale 40, Recipes—Pumpkin Pie and How to Roast a Turkey 43, Pumpkin Log 44

7 Days Until Thanksgiving..45
    The Thanksgiving Goose by Fannie Wilder Brown 46, Thanksgiving the Game 47

Contents

6 Days Until Thanksgiving..**48**
   A Mystery in the Kitchen by Olive Thorne Miller 49, Thanksgiving Song—"We Gather Together" 54

5 Days Until Thanksgiving..**55**
   Why He Carried the Turkey by James Baldwin 56, "All Good Gifts Around Us" by Matthias Claudius 56, Thanksgiving Skit 57

4 Days Until Thanksgiving..**59**
   Helen's Thanksgiving by Susan Coolidge 60, Thanksgiving Proclamation 63, Proclamation for a National Thanksgiving by George Washington 64, National Thanksgiving Proclamation by Abraham Lincoln 65

3 Days Until Thanksgiving..**67**
   Thankfullest Thanksgiving by Pauline Shackleford Colyar 68, "A Good Thanksgiving" by Marian Douglas 70, Recipes—Grandma's Angel Biscuits and Oatmeal Pie 72

2 Days Until Thanksgiving..**73**
   Turning the Thanksgiving Tables by Carolyn Sherwin Bailey 74, Thanksgiving Games—Going to Jerusalem and The Farmer in the Dell 77

1 Day Until Thanksgiving..**78**
   Squanto by Mr. Blaisdell and Mr. Ball 79, "The Landing of the Pilgrims" by Mrs. Hemans 80, Thanksgiving Songs—"We Thank Thee" 81 and "Bringing in the Sheaves" 82

Thanksgiving..**83**
   A Turkey for the Stuffing by Katherine Grace Hulbert 84, "Over the River and Through the Woods" by Lydia Maria Child 85, "The Twilight of Thanksgiving" by William D. Kelly 86, Thankful Cards 87

Index..**88**

Introduction

It is my sincere wish that this book will be used to create wonderful memories for you and your family. In our society there are so many things that vie for our attention that we often don't spend time with those we love most. A hundred years ago things were very different. Families spent time in the evenings talking, reading, singing, and just fellowshipping. With the creation of the radio things changed and when television became a staple in every home the interaction between family members decreased even more. Now with computers, movies, and a myriad of other gadgets, families spend very little time building relationships. This book has a mission to help families grow closer together.

Before you jump into this book, I have a few things I'd like to say. The book is broken up into daily sections. Each day has a story and an activity that should take about 30 to 45 minutes. The story is first but feel free to change it around and start with the activity if it works best for you. Some of the activities (such as the cooking) may take more than the allotted time, so preview the activity before you get started. Also if one of the activities doesn't sound like much fun, feel free to implement your own. If you have a special recipe you make every year, do this on one of the cooking days, or if you have a craft that you enjoy, do that on a craft day.

Nearly all the stories in this book were written in the 1800s and early 1900s so some of the language may seem old fashioned. I have modernized some of the spelling but I left most of the stories intact because the Victorian people had such a beautiful way of using words. It is always good to stretch our own vocabulary. Many of these stories have not been reprinted since their first publication and I'm so excited to share these with a whole new generation. Most of the stories can be used to help teach children important lessons. At the end of each story you could think of a few questions to ask your children, or maybe even have the children ask you questions!

Thank you for taking the time to read this introduction and I pray that your family will grow closer to each other and to God during this Thanksgiving season.

Pilgrim on a journey,
Amy Puetz

P.S. Visit www.AmyPuetz.com/Thanksgiving.html to see some other resources about Thanksgiving.

We Gather Together

We gather together to ask the Lord's blessing

He chastens and hastens His will to make known.

14 Days Until Thanksgiving

First Harvest-Home in Plymouth

By W. DeLoss Love, Jr., 1914
(adapted)

After prayer and fasting and a farewell feast, the Pilgrim fathers left the city of Leyden and sought the new and unknown land. "So they lefte ye goodly & pleasante citie," writes their historian Bradford, "which had been their resting place near twelve years, but they knew they were pilgrims and looked not much on those things, but lifted up their eyes to ye Heavens their dearest country, and quieted their spirits."

When, after many vexing days upon the deep, the Pilgrims first sighted the New World, they were filled with praise and thanksgiving. Going ashore, they fell upon their knees and blessed the God of Heaven. And after that, whenever they were delivered from accidents or despair, they gave God "solemn thanks and praise." Such were the Pilgrims and such their habit day by day.

The first winter in the New World was marked by great suffering and want. Hunger and illness thinned the little colony and caused many graves to be made on the nearby hillside.

The spring of 1621 opened. The seed was sown in the fields. The colonists cared for it without ceasing, and watched its growth with anxiety, for well they knew that their lives depended upon a full harvest.

The days of spring and summer flew by, and the autumn came. Never in Holland or England had the Pilgrims seen the like of the treasures bounteous nature now spread before them. The woodlands were arrayed in gorgeous colors, brown, crimson, and gold, and swarmed with game of all kinds that had been concealed during the summer. The little farm plots had been blessed by the sunshine and showers, and now plentiful crops stood ready for the gathering. The Pilgrims, rejoicing, reaped the fruit of their labors and housed it carefully for the winter. Then, filled with the spirit of thanksgiving, they held the first harvest-home in New England.

For one whole week they rested from work, feasted, exercised their guns, and enjoyed various recreations. Many Indians visited the colony, among these was their greatest king, Massasoit, with ninety of his braves. The Pilgrims entertained them for three days. And the Indians went out into the woods and killed fine deer, which they brought to the colony and presented to the governor and the captain and others. So all made merry together.

Bountiful was the feast! Oysters, fish, and wild turkey, Indian maize and barley bread, geese and ducks, venison and other savory meats decked the board. Kettles, skillets, and spits were overworked while knives and spoons, kindly assisted by fingers, made merry music on pewter plates. Wild grapes, "very sweete and strong," added zest to the feast. As to the vegetables, why, the good governor describes them thus:

> "All sorts of grain which our own land doth yield,
> Was hither brought, and sown in every field;
> As wheat and rye, barley, oats, beans, and peas,
> Here all thrive, and we profit from them raise.
> All sorts of roots and herbs in gardens grow,
> Parsnips, carrots, turnips, or what you'll sow,
> Onions, melons, cucumbers, radishes,
> Potatoes, beets, rhubarb, and fair cabbages."

Thus, a royal feast it was the Pilgrims spread that first golden autumn at Plymouth, a feast worthy of their Indian guests.

All slumbering discontents they smothered with common rejoicings. When the holiday was over, they were surely better, braver men because they had turned aside to rest awhile and be thankful together. So the exiles of Leyden claimed the harvests of New England.

This festival was the bursting into life of a new conception of man's dependence on God's gifts in nature. It was the promise of annual Thanksgivings to come.

The First Thanksgiving

The only reference we have to what is traditionally thought of the first Thanksgiving comes to us from Edward Winslow's *Mourt's Relation Or Journal of the Plantation at Plymouth*. In this book he writes:

Our corn did prove well, and God be praised, we had a good increase of Indian-Corn, and our barley indifferent good, but our pease not worth the gathering, for we feared they were too late sown, they came up very well, and blossomed, but the sun parched them in the blossom. Our harvest being gotten in, our governor sent four men on fowling, that so we might after a more special manner rejoice together, after we had gathered the fruit of our labors; they four in one day killed as much fowl, as with a little help beside, served the company almost a week. At which time amongst other recreations, we exercised our arms (guns), many of the Indians coming amongst us, and amongst the rest their greatest, King Massasoit, with some ninety men, whom for three days we entertained and feasted, and they went out and killed five deer, which they brought to the plantation and bestowed on our governor, and upon the captain, and others. And although it be not always so plentiful, as it was at this time with us, yet by the goodness of God, we are so far from want, that we often wish you partakers of our plenty. We have found the Indians very faithful in their covenant of peace with us; very longing and ready to pleasure us. We often go to them, and they come to us.

Activities

Harvest Hunt
by Mary Dawson, 1916

Since harvest takes place in the fall, it is only fitting to play a game that uses fresh fruit. The game may be played with any number of players.

Each player is given a basket and a list of fruit. This could include oranges, apples, plums, pears, peaches, etc. One person hides enough of each fruit to give each player one. Then the hunt begins, each player puts only one of each fruit in his or her basket. The first person to find one of each fruit wins. The prize might be the fruit or candy.

Another idea is to use something other than fruit for the hidden items. Different colored blocks, or plastic bowls or cups would work just as well. Just have a list of several different things to find.

Countdown to Thanksgiving

Make a copy of the countdown sheet (below) and mark off each day as it goes by.

13 Days Until Thanksgiving

How Obadiah Brought About Thanksgiving

By Emily Hewitt Leland, 1903

That an innocent and helpless baby should be named Obadiah Waddle was an outrage which the infant unceasingly resented from the time he was old enough to realize the awful gulf that lay between his name and those of other children. The experiences of his first day at school were branded into his soul; and although he made friends by his bright face and kind and honest nature, scarcely a day passed during his six years of village schooling without his absurd name flying out at him from some unsuspected ambush and making him cringe.

It was bad enough when the teasing came from a boy, but when a girl took to teasing or giggling at him, it seemed as if his burden was greater than he could bear. Then he would go home through the woods and fields to avoid human beings, so hurt and unhappy that nothing but his mother's greeting, and the smell of a good supper could cheer him.

At home, he had no trouble. His mother and his baby sister called him Obie, and sweet was his name on their lips. His father, who had objected to Obadiah from the first, called him Bub or Bubby; but one can bear almost any name when it comes with a loving smile or a pat on the shoulder, which was Mr. Waddle's way of addressing his only son.

Very early in life it had been explained to Obadiah that he was named for his mother's favorite brother, who gave his little namesake a silver dollar on a black silk cord before moving to California.

Obadiah often looked at this dollar, which was kept in a little box with a broken earring, a hair chain, a glass broach, and an ancient copper coin. Sometimes on circus days or on the Fourth of July he wished there was no hole in it that he might spend it on a show and lemonade or on noisy firecrackers.

But he knew that his mother valued it highly because Uncle Obie gave it to him, and because there were little dents in it made by his vigorous first teeth. So he always returned it to the box with a sigh of resignation and made the most of the twenty-five cents given him by his father on special occasions.

When he was eleven years old the Waddle family moved West, and the last thing Obadiah heard as the train pulled away from the little station of his native town was this verse, heartily shouted from a group of schoolmates assembled to bid him goodbye:

"Oh, Obadiah, you're going West,
Where the prairie winds don't have no rest,
You'll have to waddle your level best.
Goodbye, good chap, goodbye!"

Misfortune attended the Waddles in their western home. To be sure, they had their rich, broad acres, with never a stone or a stump to hinder the smooth cutting plow, but a frightful midsummer storm in the second year literally wiped out crops and cattle, and left them with their bare lives in their lowly log house.

"Drought first year, tornado second. If next year's a failure, we'll go back—if we can raise money enough to go with. Three times and then out!" said Mr. Waddle.

Mrs. Waddle broke down and wept. It scared the children to see that their mother could cry—their mother, who was always so bright and cheerful and who always laughed away their sorrows!

Mr. Waddle was scared too. He bent down and patted her shoulder—his favorite way of soothing beast or human being.

"Now, Mary, Mary! Don't you go back on us. We can stand everything as long as you are all right. Don't feel bad! We'll pick up again. There's time enough yet to grow turnips and fodder corn."

"But what will we feed it to?" wailed Mrs. Waddle.

Mr. Waddle could not answer, thinking of his splendid horses, and of his pure Jersey cows that would never answer his call again.

"Well, I am ashamed of myself!" said Mrs. Waddle, after a few moments, bravely drying her eyes. "And I'm wicked, too! I've just wished that something would happen so we'd have to go back East, and it's happened, and we might have all been killed. And I'm going to stop just where I am. I don't care where we live—or how we live—so long as we are all together—and well—and there's a crust in the house and water to drink."

Rising, she seized the broom and began vigorously to sweep together the leaves and grass which the tornado had cast in through the open door.

"I declare, Mary!" said Mr. Waddle. "Do you mean to say you've been homesick all this time?"

"I'd give more for the north side of one of those old Vermont hills than I would for the whole prairie," was the emphatic reply. "But I'm not going to say another single word."

Mr. Waddle felt a thrill of comfort in knowing he was not alone in his yearning for the old home. It was singular that these two, who loved each other so truly, could so hide their inmost feelings. Each had feared to appear weak to the other.

Mr. Waddle looked at his wife with almost a radiant smile. "Well, Mary, we'll go back in the fall—if we can sell. I guess we can hire the Deacon Elbridge's place I see by last week's paper it's still for sale or rent, and carpenter work in old Hartbridge is about as profitable for me as farming out West."

"I'm glad you wouldn't mind going back, Homer," said Mrs. Waddle, and they looked at each other as in the days of their courtship.

But selling the farm was not easy, and October found the Waddles in painful straits.

"What will we have for Thanksgiving, Ma?" asked Obadiah.

"Oh, a pair of nice prairie chickens, mashed turnips, hot biscuits, and melted sugar," cheerfully replied Mrs. Waddle.

"That sounds pretty good," said Obadiah; but when he got out of doors he said to himself that you could not shoot prairie chickens without ammunition, and that he had no bait even if he tried to use his quail traps. He also reflected that his mother looked thin and pale, that sister Ellie needed shoes, and that plum pudding and mince pie used to be on Thanksgiving tables. But this was the day for his run to the post office—which seemed to cheer him up somehow.

When he went to town for the mail, he would see if his father, who was at work carpentering on a barn, could not spare a dime for a little powder and shot. So the boy trudged away on his long walk, with his empty gun on his shoulder and the hope of youth in his heart.

His father, busy at work, greeted him cheerily but had no dime for powder and shot. Pay for the work was not to be had until the first of December, and meanwhile every penny must be saved—for coal and for Ellie's shoes.

"It leaves Thanksgiving out in the cold, doesn't it, Bub? But we'll make it up at Christmas, maybe," said Mr. Waddle, as Obadiah turned to go. "Here's three cents for a bite of candy for Sis, and take good care of Mother. I'll be home day after tomorrow, likely."

Obadiah jingled the three pennies in his pocket as he walked to the combined store and post office. Three cents! They would buy a charge or two of powder and shot, and he still had a few caps. And candy was not good for people anyhow! He wished he had asked his father if he might buy ammunition instead.

"But I'll not bother him again," he decided, "and Sis will be glad enough of the candy."

He would not buy rashly. He looked over the jars of striped sticks, peppermint drops, chocolate candies, and mixed varieties. Then he sat down on a nail keg to await the distribution of the mail. He watched the people standing by for the opening of the delivery window. It was a rare thing for his family to get a letter, but then they seldom sent one.

Once in a while a newspaper came from Uncle Obadiah, but only one letter in two years. Perhaps if he knew what hard times they were having, he would write oftener. The boy had heard his mother say only the week before that she wanted to write to Brother Obie, but was no hand at letters, especially when there was no good news to write.

A thought now came to young Obadiah. He would write to his Uncle tomorrow, and his brain began fairly to hum with what he would say. When his time came, he invested one cent in a clean white stick of candy and the remaining two in a postage stamp. "I'll pay two cents back to Pa as soon as I get the answer," he said confidently to his questioning conscience.

His walk home abounded in exasperations. Never had game appeared so plentiful. Three separate flocks of prairie chickens flew directly over his head, a rabbit scurried across his path, and in the stubble of the ruined grain fields rose and fell little clouds of quail.

"They just know it ain't loaded!" grumbled Obadiah, trudging with his empty gun.

That night, after Sis had gone to sleep, and his mother had lain down beside her, cheerfully remarking that bed was cheaper than fire, and that she was glad there was a good wood lot on the Elbridge place, Obadiah, behind the sheltering canvas partition that separated the kitchen from the bedrooms, wrote the following letter:

Dear Uncle,

Last year our crops were burned up by the drought and this year they were swept away by a cyclone and all the stock was killed, and Father will not get his pay for carpenter work until December. If there was no hole in the dollar you gave me when I was a baby, I would take it and buy something for Thanksgiving. I wish you would send me a dollar without a hole in it as soon as you can and I will send you the one with a hole in it. I would send it now, but I have not got stamps enough. I hope you are well. We are all well, only Ma is homesick.

Your sincere nephew,
Obadiah Waddle

P. S. Please send your answer right to me, because I want to surprise Ma with some things for Thanksgiving.

The next morning he set off to look at his most distant quail traps, found them empty, and circled round to the village, where he posted his letter.

The days crept slowly by, and times grew more and more uncomfortable in the little log house. Often when Obadiah was doing his "sums" his pencil would shy off to a corner of his slate and scribble a list of items something like this:

2 cents to Pa	$0.02
Stamps and paper (to send the D)	$0.06
Powder and shot	$0.10
Tea and sugar for Ma	$0.30
1 lb. raisins	$0.15
6 eggs	$0.08
1 lb. butter	$0.20
	$0.91
More powder	$0.09
	$1.00

Sometimes he would set down half a pound of "raisins" and add "candy for Sis, five cents," but this was in his reckless moments. A sober second thought always convinced him that "raisins" would bring the greatest good to the greatest number about Thanksgiving time.

He casually asked his mother how long it took people to go to California.

"Well, Uncle Obie's newspapers always get here about four or five days after they are printed. Dear me! I must write to your Uncle Obie just as soon as we can spare the money for paper and stamps. He'll be glad to know we are all alive and well, and that's about all I can tell him."

Obadiah smiled broadly behind his geography and began reckoning the days. The answer might arrive about the eighteenth, but he heroically waited until the twenty-first before going to ask for it. He reached the village long before mail time, but saw so many things to consider in the grocery and provision line that he was almost surprised when the rattle of the mail rig and a gathering of people told that the important time had arrived.

The Waddles had given up their box, so he could not expect to see his letter until it should be handed out to him from the general "W" pile. He waited patiently. The fortunate owners of lock boxes took out their letters with a proud air while the distributing was still going on. Others, who had mere open boxes, drew close and tried to read illegible superscriptions with poor success. Others who never had either letters or papers but who came in at this hour from force of habit, stood near the stove or leaned on the counters and spoke of the weather and swapped feeble jokes. Finally, the small wooden window was flung open. The little group got its papers and letters and gradually retired.

"Any letter for me?" cried Obadiah, his heart jumping.

"Nope; your pa got your papers last Saturday."

"But—ain't there a letter—for me?"

The man hastily ran over the half-dozen "W" envelopes. "Nope."

Obadiah's heart was heavy as lead now. He went out into the sleety weather and faced the long walk home. His eyes were so blurred with tears he could hardly see, and his feet came near slipping.

A derisive shout came from across the street, "Hallo! Pretty bad 'waddling' this weather!"

Obadiah pulled his hat over his eyes and tramped on in scornful silence.

And now another voice called out to him, a voice from the rear, "Oh, say! Waddle! Come back here—package for ye!" Obadiah hastily went back, his heart leaping.

"Registered package," explained the postmaster. "'Most forgot it. Sign your name on that line. Odd name you've got. No danger your mail going to some other fellow."

Obadiah laughed and said he guessed not, and hardly believing his senses, again started for home, and soon struck out upon the far-stretching road. The clouds had lifted, and a feeble sun was vainly trying to regain supremacy. In the privacy of the great prairie, he looked at the package again. How heavy it was for such a small one, and how important looked the long row of stamps; and there was Uncle Obadiah's name in one corner, proving that it was truly the answer!

There must be a jackknife in it or something besides the dollar. He cut the stout twine, removed the wrapper, and lifted the cover of a strong paper box. There was something wrapped in neat white paper and feeling very solid.

Obadiah removed the paper, and a heavy, handsome and very fat leather purse slipped into his hand. He opened it. It had several compartments, and in each one were three or more hard, flat, round objects wrapped in more white paper to keep them from jingling, very likely.

Obadiah unwrapped one of these round, flat objects, and even in the dull light of the fading November day he could see that it was a bright, clean, shining silver dollar—and had no hole in it.

With hands fairly shaking with joy, he returned the purse to the box and sped homeward. He ran all the way, only slowing up for breath now and then, but it was dark, and the poor little supper was waiting when he reached the house. The small lamp did not shed a very brilliant light, but a mother does not need an electric glare in order to read her child's face.

"Well, Obie, what's happened?" asked his mother as soon as he was inside the door. "Have you caught a whole flock of quails?"

"Something better 'n quails! Guess again, Ma!"

"Three nice fat prairie hens then?"

"Something better 'n prairie hens." And then Obie could wait no longer. He pulled the package from under his coat and tossed it down beside the poor old teapot, which had known little but hot water these many weeks.

"Why, it's from Brother Obie—to you!" exclaimed his mother, while his father drew near and said, "Well, well!"

"And look inside! I haven't half looked yet," said Obie, "but you look, Ma! I just want you to look!"

Ma opened the box, and then the purse, and then the fourteen round objects wrapped in white paper. And they made a fine glitter on the red tablecloth.

"Well, well!" repeated Mr. Waddle.

"And here's something written," said Mrs. Waddle, taking a paper from a pocket at the back of the purse.

"Read it, Ma—out loud! I don't care," said Obie generously.

So Ma read it in a voice that trembled a little:

My Dear Nephew,

    If I count rightly, it is thirteen years since your good mother labeled you Obadiah. I'm not near enough to give you thirteen slaps—I wish I were—so I send you thirteen dollars, and one to grow on. Never mind returning the dollar with the hole in it—keep it for your grandchildren to cut their teeth on. Give my love to your parents and little sister, and if you look the purse through closely, I think you will find something of interest to your mother. It is about time she paid our old Vermont a visit. Be a good boy.

                              Your affectionate uncle,
                              Obadiah Brown

"Oh, that blessed brother!" cried Mrs. Waddle, wiping her eyes with her apron.

Obie seized the purse and examined it on all sides. It was a very special purse, for another little flat pocket was found in its inmost center, and from it Obie drew out another bit of folded paper and opened it.

"Why, it's a check!" shouted Mr. Waddle. "A check for you, Mary, for—two—hundred—dollars! My! There's a brother for you!"

"Oh, not two hundred—it must be twenty—it can't be—" faltered Mrs. Waddle, wiping her eyes to look at the paper.

Then she gave a little cry and fell to hugging all her family. "We can all go back—we can go next week!" and she almost danced up and down on the unresponsive clay floor.

"I owe you two cents, Pa, and I'll pay it back to you just as soon as I can get a dollar changed," said Obadiah proudly, fingering the shining coins.

"How's that, Bubby?"

Then Obadiah explained.

"I hope you didn't complain, Obie," said his mother, her happy face clouding.

"Well, I told him about the drought and the cyclone. I guess if I was a near relation I wouldn't call that complaining. And then I asked him if he wouldn't swap dollars with me, so I could have one without a hole in it to get something for Thanks—"

Mr. Waddle broke in with a shout of laughter, and Mrs. Waddle kissed her son once more, and laughed, too, although her eyes were full of tears. And then Obadiah knew everything was all right.

"We can have Thanksgiving now, can't we, Ma?" he asked. "It's so near, and I'm going to get all the things. We'll have chicken pie—tame chicken pie—and plum pudding—and butter—and cream for the coffee—and cranberries—and lump sugar—and pumpkin pie—and—"

"Oh, me wants supper!" exclaimed Sis. And then they laughed again and fell upon the cooling cornbread and molasses and melancholy bits of fried pork and the thin tea as if they were already engaged in a feast of Thanksgiving. And so they were.

We Thank Thee
by Ralph Waldo Emerson

For flowers that bloom about our feet;
For tender grass, so fresh, so sweet;
For song of bird, and hum of bee;
For all things fair we hear or see.
Father in heaven, we thank Thee!
For blue of stream and blue of sky;
For pleasant shade of branches high;
For fragrant air and cooling breeze;
For beauty of the blooming trees,
Father in heaven, we thank Thee!

Thanksgiving Song

Sing the song on the next page and discuss what it means. "Count Your Blessings" is a good reminder to think about the truly important things God has given us.

Count Your Blessings

12 Days Until Thanksgiving

The Soap Making of Remember Biddle

By Carolyn Sherwin Bailey, 1917

"It may chance that you will not be able to return by Thanksgiving Day?" Remember Biddle asked with almost a sob in her voice.

A little Puritan girl of long ago was Remember, dressed in a long straight gown of gray stuff, heavy hobnailed shoes and wearing a white kerchief crossed about her neck. She stood in the door of the little log farmhouse that looked out upon the dreary stretch of the Atlantic coast with Plymouth Rock raising its gray head not so very far away.

No wonder Remember felt unhappy. Her mother was at the door, mounted upon their horse, and ready to start away for quite a long journey as journeys were counted in those days. She was going with a bundle of herbs to care for a sick neighbor who lived a distance of ten miles away. It had been an urgent summons, brought by the post carrier that morning. The neighbor was ill, indeed, and the fame of Mistress Biddle's herb brewing was well known through the countryside.

She leaned down from the saddle to touch Remember's dark braids. The little girl had run out beside the horse and laid her cheek against his soft side. Her father was far away in Boston, attending to some important matters of shipping. Her mother's going left Remember all alone.

She repeated her question, "Shall I be alone for Thanksgiving Day, Mother, Dear?" she asked.

Her mother turned away that the little daughter might not see that her eyes, as well, were full of sorrow.

"I know not, Remember. I sent a letter this morning by the post carrier to Boston telling your father that I should wait for him at Neighbor Allison's, and if I could leave the poor woman he could come home with me. I hope that we shall be here in time for Thanksgiving Day, but if it should happen, Remember, that you must be alone, take no thought of your loneliness. Think only of how much cause we have for being thankful in this free, fertile land of New England. And keep busy, dear child. You will find plenty to do in the house until my return."

Throwing the girl a goodbye kiss, Mistress Biddle gave the horse a light touch with her riding whip and was off down the road, her long, dark cloak blowing like a gray cloud on the horizon in the chilly November wind.

For a few moments Remember leaned against the beams of the door listening to the call of a flock of flying crows and the crackling of the dried cornstalks in the field back of the house. Beyond the cornfield lay the brown and green woods, uncut, save by an occasional winding Indian trail. The neighboring cabins were so far away that they looked like toy houses set on the edge of other fields of dried cornstalks. Looking again toward the woods Remember shivered a little. She saw in imagination, a tall, dark figure in bright blanket and trailing feather headdress stalk out from the depths of the thicket of pines and oaks. Then she laughed.

"There hasn't been an Indian passed here since early in the summer," she said to herself. "Mother would not have left me here alone if she had not known that I should be quite safe. I will go in now and play that I am the mistress of this house, and I am getting it ready for company on Thanksgiving Day. It will be so much fun that I shall forget all about being a lonely little girl.

It was a happy play. Remember tied one of her mother's long aprons over her dress to keep it clean and began her busy work of cleaning the house and making it shine from cellar to ceiling. She sorted the piles of ruddy apples and winter squashes and pumpkins in the cellar and rehung the slabs of rich bacon and the strings of onions. As she touched the bundles of savory herbs that hung about the cellar walls, Remember gave a little sigh.

"I see no chance of these being used in the stuffing of a fat turkey for Thanksgiving," she said to herself. "It may be that I shall have to eat nothing but mush and apple sauce for my dinner, and all alone. Ah, well-a-day!" She began to sing in her sweet, child voice one of the hymns that she had learned at the big white meetinghouse:

> "The Lord is both my health and light;
> Shall men make me dismayed?
> Since God doth give me strength and might,
> Why should I be afraid?"

As she sang, Remember lifted a bucket of soft soap that stood on the cellar floor and tugged it up to the kitchen. Then she went to work with a will.

Several days passed before Remember had cleaned the house to her satisfaction. On her hands and knees she scoured the floors, her rosy hands and arms drenched with the foaming soapsuds. Afterward, she sprinkled sand upon the spotless boards in pretty patterns as was the fashion in those days. She swept the brick hearth with a broom made of twigs, and she scoured the pewter and copper utensils until they were as bright as so many mirrors. She washed the wooden chairs until the bunch of cherries painted upon the back of each looked bright enough to pick and eat. She dusted the straight rush-bottomed chairs and the bench that stood by the side of the fireplace. Even the tall clock in the corner had its round glass face washed. Then Remember stood in the center of the kitchen looking at the good result of her work.

"My mother, herself, could have done no better!" she thought. Then she looked at the keg that had held their precious store of soft soap. There was no soap to be bought in those long-ago days; the Puritans were obliged to make their own.

"I have used up all the soap. Oh, what will my mother say at such waste? What shall I do?" Remember said, in dismay.

She sat down by the fire and thought. Suddenly she jumped up. A happy plan had come to her.

"I will make a mess of soap," Remember said to herself. "I have helped mother to make soap many a time and I can do no more than try. It is yet some days until Thanksgiving and I should be sadly idle with nothing more to do, now that the house is put so well in order."

The soap-making barrel, a hole bored in the bottom, stood in a corner of the cellar; it was light enough so that Remember could easily handle it and she was strong for her twelve summers and winters. In the bottom of the barrel she put a layer of clean, fresh straw from the shed and over this she filled the barrel as far as she could with wood ashes. Then she rolled, and tugged, and lifted the barrel to a high bench that stood by the kitchen door, taking care that the hole was just above a large, empty bucket. Then Remember brought pails of water and, standing on a stool, poured the water into the barrel until it began to drip down through the ashes and the straw into the bucket below. It looked rather dirty as it filtered down into the bucket but Remember took good care not to touch it with her fingers for she knew that it had turned into lye. Late in the afternoon Remember took out a hen's egg and dropped it into the bucket to see what would happen.

"It floats!" she said. "Now I am sure that I made the lye right and I can attend to the grease tomorrow."

Remember had to start a huge fire the next day and she got out the great black soap kettle, filled it with the lye and hung it over the fire. Into this she put many scraps of meat fat and waste grease that her mother had been saving for just such a soap-making emergency as this. It bubbled and boiled and Remember carefully skimmed from the top all the bones and skin and pieces of candle wicking that rose, as the lye absorbed the grease, and cooked it into a thick, ropy mixture. It looked very much like molasses candy as it boiled and after a while Remember knew that it was done. She lifted the kettle off the fire and poured the thick, brown jelly, that was now good soft soap, into big earthenware crocks to cool.

"I made the soap quite as well as my mother could," Remember said to herself with a great deal of satisfaction as she put the crocks, all save one, in the cellar. This one she kept for use in the kitchen.

"There's not another thing that I can think of to do," Remember said now. She looked out of the window at the bleak, bare fields behind which the November sun was just preparing to set in a flame-colored ball. "Here it is the afternoon before Thanksgiving Day and Mother and Father are not home yet, and we haven't anything in the house for a Thanksgiving dinner!" She looked toward the woods now. What was that?

A speck of color that she could see in the narrow footpath between the trees suddenly came nearer, growing larger and brighter all the time. Remember could distinguish the colorful blanket, bright moccasins, and feather headdress of an Indian. Stalking across the field, he was fast approaching their little log house which he could easily see from the woods and which seemed to offer him an easy goal. Remember covered her face with her hands, trying in her terror to think what to do.

The bolt on the kitchen door was but a flimsy protection at best. Remember knew that the Indian would be able to wrench it off with one tug of his brawny arm. She knew, too, that it had been the custom of the Indians who were encamped not far off to take the children of the colonists and hold them for a high ransom.

"The white face takes our lands. We take the papoose of the white face," they had threatened, and they were cruel indeed to the children whom they held, especially if their parents were a long time supplying the necessary ransom. But it had been so long since an Indian had been seen in their little settlement, that Remember's mother had felt quite safe in leaving her.

Remember looked now for a place to hide. There was none. The cellar would be the first place, she knew, the Indian would look for her. The tall clock was too small a space into which to squeeze her plump little body; and there was no use hiding under the bed for she would be dragged out at once. Remember turned, now, hearing a footstep. The Indian, big, brown, and frowning had crossed the threshold and stood in the center of the room. His blanket trailed the floor; over his shoulder was slung a pair of wild turkeys he had killed.

Remember trembled, but she faced him bravely.

"Greetings," she said, reaching out a kind little hand to him. The Indian shook his head and did not offer to shake hands with the little girl. Instead, he pointed to the door, motioning to her that she was to follow him.

Remember's mind worked quickly. She knew that Indians were fond of trinkets and could sometimes be turned away from their cruel designs by means of very small gifts. She ran to her mother's work basket and offered him in succession a pair of scissors, a case of bright, new needles, a scarlet pincushion, and a silver thimble. Each, in turn, the Indian refused, shaking his head and still indicating by his gestures that Remember was to follow him.

Now he grasped the little girl's hand and tried to pull her. There was no use resisting. But just as they reached the door the Indian caught sight of the crock of soft soap—dark, sticky, and strangely fascinating to him. He stuck one long brown finger in it and started to put it in his mouth, but Remember reached up and pulled his hand away. She shook her head and made a wry face to show him that it was not good to eat.

"How?" he questioned, pointing to the soap.

Remember pulled from his grasp. Pouring a dipperful of water in a basin, she took a handful of the soap and showed the Indian how she could wash her hands. As he watched a look, first of wonder, and then of pleasure, crept into his face. He smiled and looked at his own hands. They were stained with earth and sadly in need of washing. Remember refilled the basin with water and the Indian, helping himself to a huge handful of the soap, washed his hands solemnly as if it were a kind of ceremony.

As Remember watched him, her heart beat fast indeed. "As soon as he finishes he will take me away," she thought.

Slowly the Indian dried his hands on the towel she gave him. Then he picked up the crock of soft soap. He set it on his shoulder. Pointing to the pair of turkeys that he had laid on the table to show that he was giving them to Remember in exchange for the soap, he strode out of the door and was soon lost to sight in the wood's path.

Remember dropped down in a chair and could scarcely believe she was really safe. A quick clatter of hoofs roused her. She darted to the door.

"Father, Mother!" she cried.

Yes, it was indeed! Her father riding in front with her mother in the saddle behind.

"Just in time for Thanksgiving!" they cried as they jumped down and embraced Remember.

"And I'm here, too, and we have a pair of turkeys for dinner," Remember said, half smiles and half tears, as she told them her strange adventure.

Thanksgiving Quiz

See how much you know about Thanksgiving. Answers are below.

True or False?

1. The Pilgrims dressed in black and white clothing.
2. Thanksgiving was celebrated in all parts of the country after the first Thanksgiving.
3. The Pilgrims planned to settle in Virginia.
4. The Pilgrims' Thanksgiving celebration was the first held in North America.
5. George Washington issued a Thanksgiving Proclamation in 1789.
6. Abraham Lincoln issued a Thanksgiving Proclamation in 1863.
7. The woman who helped make Thanksgiving a national holiday was Martha Washington.
8. In 1941, Congress officially set the first Thursday in November as Thanksgiving day.

Answers 1. False, they actually wore bright colored clothes. 2. False, it did not become popular until the 1800s. 3. True, they were blown off course. 4. False, there is evidence of several other celebrations. 5. True. 6. True. 7. False, it was Sarah Hale. 8. False, it was the fourth Thursday in November.

11 Days Until Thanksgiving

Davy's Thanksgiving

By J. T. Trowbridge, 1915

At noon on a dreary November day, a lonesome little fellow, looking very red about the ears and very blue about the mouth, stood kicking his heels at the door of a cheap eating house in Boston, and offering a solitary copy of a morning paper for sale to the people passing.

But there were really not many people passing, for it was Thanksgiving Day, and the shops were shut, and everybody who had a home to go to and a dinner to eat seemed to have gone home to eat that dinner, while Davy Hampton, the newsboy, stood trying in vain to sell the last "extry" left on his hands by the slow business of the morning.

An old man, with a face that looked pinched and who was dressed in a worn black coat and a much-battered stovepipe hat, stopped at the same doorway, and with one hand on the latch, appeared to hesitate between hunger and the poor paperboy before him.

It was possible, however, that he was considering whether he could afford himself the indulgence of a morning paper (seeing it was Thanksgiving Day); so, at least, Davy thought, and accosted him accordingly.

"Buy a paper, sir? All about the fire in East Boston, and arrest of safe-burglars in Springfield. Only two cents!"

The little old man looked at the boy with keen gray eyes, which seemed to light up the pinched and skinny face, and answered in a shrill voice that whistled through white front teeth, "You ought to come down in your price this time of day. You can't expect to sell a morning paper at twelve o'clock for full price."

"Well, give me a cent then," said Davy. "That's less'n cost; but never mind; I'm bound to sell out anyhow."

"You look cold," said the old man.

"Cold?" replied Davy. "I'm froze. And I want my dinner. And I'm going to have a big dinner, too, seeing it's Thanksgiving Day."

"Ah! You are fortunate, my boy!" said the old man. "You've a home to go to, and friends too, I hope?"

"No, sir; nary home, and nary friend; only my mother and sisters"—Davy hesitated, and grew serious; then suddenly changed his tone—"and Hop Houghton. I told him to meet me here, and we'd have a first-rate Thanksgiving dinner together. For it's no fun to be eatin' alone Thanksgiving Day! It sets a feller thinking of everything, if he ever had a home and then hain't got a home anymore."

"It's more lonesome not to eat at all," said the old man, his gray eyes twinkling. "And what can a boy like you have to think of? Here, I guess I can find one cent for you, though there's nothing in the paper, I know."

The old man spoke with some feeling; his fingers trembled, and somehow he dropped two cents instead of one into Davy's hand.

"Here! You've made a mistake!" cried Davy. "A bargain's a bargain. You've given me a cent too much."

"No, I didn't. I never give anybody a cent too much."

"But, see here!" and Davy showed the two cents, offering to return one.

"No matter," said the old man, "it will be so much less for my dinner, that's all."

Davy had instinctively pocketed the pennies when, on a moment's reflection, his sympathies were excited.

"Poor old man!" he thought, "he's seen better days I guess. Perhaps he's no home. A boy like me can stand it, but I guess it must be hard for him. He meant to give me the odd cent all the while, and I don't believe he has had a decent dinner for many a day."

All this, which I have been obliged to write out slowly in words, went through Davy's mind like a flash. He was a generous little fellow, and any kindness shown him, no matter how trifling, made his heart overflow.

"Look here!" he cried, "where are you going to get your dinner today?"

"I can get a bite here as well as anywhere. It don't matter much to me," replied the old man.

"Dine with me," said Davy, laughing. "I'd like to have you."

"I'm afraid I couldn't afford to dine as you are going to," said the man, with a smile, his eyes twinkling again and his white front teeth shining.

"I'll pay for your dinner!" Davy exclaimed. "Come! We don't have a Thanksgiving but once a year, and a feller wants a good time then."

"But you are waiting for another boy."

"Oh, Hop Houghton! He won't come now. It's so late. He's gone to a place down in North Street, I guess—a place I don't like. There's so much tobacco smoked and so much beer drank there." Davy cast a final glance up the street. "No, he won't come now. So much the worse for him! He likes the men down there, I don't."

"Ah!" said the man, taking off his hat, and giving it a brush with his elbow, as they entered the restaurant, as if trying to appear as respectable as he could in the eyes of a newsboy of such fastidious tastes.

To make him feel quite comfortable in his mind on that point, Davy hastened to say, "I mean rowdies, and such. Poor people, if they behave themselves, are just as respectable to me as rich folks. I ain't the least mite aristocratic."

"Ah, indeed!" And the old man smiled again and seemed to look relieved. "I'm very glad to hear it."

He placed his hat on a wall peg and took a seat opposite Davy at a little table, which they had all to themselves.

Davy offered him the bill of fare.

"No, I must ask you to choose for me, but nothing very extravagant, you know. I'm used to plain fare," the man said.

"So am I. But I'm going to have a good dinner for once in my life, and so shall you," cried Davy, generously. "What do you say to chicken soup, and then wind up with a thumping big piece of squash pie? How's that for a Thanksgiving dinner?"

"Sumptuous," said the old man, appearing to glow with the warmth of the room and the prospect of a good dinner. "But won't it cost you too much?"

"Too much? No, Sir!" laughed Davy. "Chicken soup, fifteen cents; pie—they give tremendous pieces here, thick, I tell you—ten cents. That's twenty-five cents; half a dollar for two. Of course, I don't do this way every day in the year. But mother's glad to have me enjoy myself once in a while. Here, waiter!" And Davy gave his princely order as if he did it everyday.

"Where is your mother? Why don't you dine with her?" the little man asked.

Davy's face grew serious in a moment.

"That's the question. Why don't I? I'll tell you why I don't. I've got the best mother in the world. What I'm trying to do is to make a home for her, so we can live together and eat our Thanksgiving dinners together some time. Some boys want one thing, some another. Some goes in for good times; another's in such a hurry to get rich he don't care much how he does it. But what I want most of anything is to be with my mother and my two sisters again, and I ain't ashamed to say so."

Davy's eyes grew very tender, and he went on, while his companion across the table watched him with a very gentle, searching look.

"I haven't been with her now for nearly two years, hardly at all since Father died. When his business was settled up—he kept a little grocery store on Hanover Street—it was found he hadn't left us anything. We had lived pretty well up to that time, and I and my two sisters had been to school; but then Mother had to do something, and her friends got her places to go out nursing, and she's a nurse now. Everybody likes her, and she has enough to do. We couldn't be with her, of course. She got us boarded at a good place, but I saw how hard it was going to be for her to support us, so I said, 'I'm a boy; I can do something for myself. You just pay their board, and keep 'em to school, and I'll go to work, and maybe help you a little, besides taking care of myself.'"

"What could you do?" said the little old man.

"That's it. I was only eleven years old, and what could I do? What I should have liked would have been some nice place where I could do light work and stand a chance of learning a good business. But beggars mustn't be choosers. I couldn't find such a place, and I wasn't going to be loafing about the streets, so I went to selling newspapers. I've sold newspapers ever since, and I shall be thirteen years old next month."

"You like it?" said the old man.

"I like to get my own living," replied Davy proudly, "but what I want is to learn some trade, or regular business, and settle down, and make a home for—but there's no use talking about that. Make the best of things, that's my motto. Don't this soup smell good? And don't it taste good, too? They haven't put so much chicken in yours as they have in mine. If you don't mind my having tasted it, we'll change."

The old man declined this liberal offer, took Davy's advice to help himself freely to bread, which "didn't cost anything," and ate his soup with prodigious relish, as it seemed to Davy, who grew more and more hospitable and patronizing as the repast proceeded.

"Come, now, won't you have something between the soup and the pie? Don't be shy. I'll pay for it. Thanksgiving don't come but once a year. You won't? A cup of tea, then, to go with your pie?"

"I think I will have a cup of tea. You are so kind," said the old man.

"All right! Here, waiter! Two pieces of your fattest and biggest squash pie, and a cup of tea, strong, for this gentleman."

"I've told you about myself," added Davy; "suppose, now, you tell me something."

"About myself?"

"Yes. I think that would go pretty well with the pie."

But the man shook his head. "I could go back and tell about my plans and hopes when I was a lad of your age, but it would be too much like your own story over again. Life isn't what we think it will be when we are young. You'll find that out soon enough. I am all alone in the world now, and I am sixty-seven years old."

"Have some cheese with your pie, won't you? It must be so lonely at your age! What do you do for a living?"

"I have a little place in Devonshire Street. My name is Crooker. You'll find me up two flights of stairs, back room, at the right. Come and see me, and I'll tell you all about my business, and perhaps help you to such a place as you want, for I know several business men. Now don't fail."

And Mr. Crooker wrote his address with a little stub of a pencil on a corner of the newspaper which had led to their acquaintance, tore it off carefully, and gave it to Davy.

Thereupon the latter took a card from his pocket, not a very clean one, I must say (I am speaking of the card, though the remark will apply equally well to the pocket) and handed it across the table to his new friend.

"David Hampton, Dealer in Newspapers," the old man read, with his sharp gray eyes, which glanced up funnily at Davy, seeming to say, "Isn't this rather aristocratic for a twelve-year-old newsboy?"

Davy blushed and explained, "Got up for me by a printer's boy I know. I'd done some favors for him, so he made me a few cards. Handy to have sometimes, you know."

"Well, David," said the little old man, "I'm glad to have made your acquaintance. The pie was excellent, thank you—and I hope you'll come and see me. You'll find me in very humble quarters, but you are not aristocratic, you say. Now won't you let me pay for my dinner? I believe I have money enough. Let me see."

Davy would not hear of such a thing, but walked up to the desk and settled the bill with the air of a person who regarded it as a trifling expense.

When he looked around again, the little old man was gone.

"Never mind, I'll go and see him the first chance I have," said Davy, as he looked at the penciled strip of newspaper margin again before putting it into his pocket.

He then went round to his miserable quarters, in the top of a cheap lodging-house, where he made himself ready, by means of soap and water and a broken comb, to walk five miles into the suburbs and get a sight, if only for five minutes, of his mother.

On the following Monday, Davy, having a leisure hour, went to call on his new acquaintance in Devonshire Street.

Having climbed the two flights, he found the door of the back room at the right ajar, and looking in, saw Mr. Crooker at a desk, in the act of receiving a roll of money from a well-dressed visitor.

Davy entered unnoticed and waited until the money was counted, and a receipt signed. Then, as the visitor departed, old Mr. Crooker looked round and saw Davy. He offered him a chair, then turned to lock up the money in a safe.

"So this is your place of business?" said Davy, glancing about the plain office room. "What do you do here?"

"I buy real estate sometimes—sell—rent—and so forth."

"Who for?" asked Davy.

"For myself," said little old Mr. Crooker, with a smile.

Davy stared, perfectly aghast at the situation. This, then, was the man whom he had invited to dinner, and treated so patronizingly the preceding Thursday!

"I—I thought—you was a poor man."

"I am a poor man," said Mr. Crooker, locking his safe. "Money doesn't make a man rich. I've money enough. I own houses in the city. They give me something to think of, and so keep me alive. I had truer riches once, but I lost them long ago."

From the way the old man's voice trembled and eyes glistened, Davy thought he must have meant by these riches friends he had lost—wife and children, perhaps.

"To think of me inviting you to dinner!" the boy cried, abashed and ashamed.

"It was odd." And Mr. Crooker showed his white front teeth with a smile. "But it may turn out to have been a fortunate circumstance for both of us. I like you. I believe in you, and I've an offer to make to you. I want a trusty, bright boy in this office, somebody I can bring up to my business, and leave it with, as I get too old to attend to it myself. What do you say?"

What could Davy say?

Again that afternoon he walked—or rather, ran—to his mother, and after consulting with her, joyfully accepted Mr. Crooker's offer.

Interviews between his mother and his employer soon followed, resulting in something for which at first the boy had not dared to hope. The lonely, childless old man, who owned so many houses, wanted a cheerful woman to keep house for him. Davy and his two sisters were requested to accompany their mother.

Of course, this proposition was accepted, and Davy soon had the satisfaction of seeing the great ambition of his youth accomplished. He had employment which promised to become a profitable business (as indeed it did in a few years, he and the old man proved so useful to each other); and, more than that, he was united once more with his mother and sisters in a happy home where he has since had a good many Thanksgiving dinners.

Thanksgiving Before the Pilgrims
By William S. Walsh, 1898

The celebration of Thanksgiving has a long and curious history. Days set apart for special thanksgiving to the Lord were known to the Israelites, and are mentioned throughout the Bible. The Greeks and Egyptians also held fall festivals of thanksgiving. They were not uncommon in England and Scotland before the Reformation and among Protestants afterwards.

Possibly the first thanksgiving held in North America was conducted by an English minister named Wolfall, in the year 1578, on the shores of Newfoundland. The reverend gentleman accompanied the expedition under Frobisher which brought the first English colony to settle on these shores. The records of this day's observances are thus preserved in the ship's log, "On Monday morning, May 27, 1578, aboard the Ayde we received all the communion by the minister of Gravesend and prepared as good Christians toward God and resolute men for all fortunes and toward night we departed toward Tilberry Hope. Here we highly praised God and altogether upon our knees gave Him due humble and hearty thanks, and Maister Wolfall, a learned man appointed by her Majesty's council to be our minister, made unto us a godlye sermon, exhorting all especially to be thankful to God for His strange and miraculous deliverance in those dangerous places." This was perhaps the first Christian sermon preached and the first celebration of the Holy Communion in North America.

The earliest record of any observance of a similar service within the present territory of the United States was held by the explorer Coronado in 1541. He is said to have held a feast with the Teya Indians in Texas.

But these were mere thanksgiving services, which only consumed a few hours and did not color the whole day. The real origin of Thanksgiving as a day specially set apart for prayer and rejoicing must be attributed to Governor Bradford, the first governor of Massachusetts Colony. In gratitude for the plentiful harvest of 1621, following upon a period of great depression, he proclaimed a day of thanksgiving to be observed on December 13 of that year.

Thanksgiving Song

Sing the song on the next page and discuss what it means.

Harvest Hymn

A Russian Folksong

Countdown to Thanksgiving — 26 — Amy Puetz

10 Days Until Thanksgiving

Captain Christy's Thanksgiving
By Carolyn Sherwin Bailey, 1918

"You're going beyond the lifeline, and the water's so rough you'll never be able to swim. Oh, Donald, don't! Come back. Don't go out so far!" The voice of the boy's little sister, Nan, shrilled out over the singing surf and was lost before it reached him.

The water of the swimming beach at Fishers Point was temptingly warm for so late in the season. Inside the boundaries of the safety line that the coast guard had stretched to mark the danger line there was a crowd of merry swimmers. No one heard Nan's warning to her brother. No one saw his brown head bobbing on the far side of the rope or noticed his arm waved above the surf in a happy challenge and goodbye. Donald was always daring in sport, but fighting ocean breakers was hard for a twelve-year-old boy who could count his strokes in still water. For a moment his white face showed above the waves. Then Donald disappeared from sight.

"Donald! Oh, save my brother, Donald!" Nan cried, plowing her way through the foam and up the beach.

"Boy gone down! Where is the coast guard? Going beyond the lifeline, and he's gone down twice." The crowd knew now, and shouted, and made futile efforts to get out to him.

But a slim, gray boat suddenly swung out to sea from the upper end of the beach, nosing its way among the white caps like a setter scenting a fresh trail. It was manned and rowed by a crew of four sailors who sent it flying to the rescue. In its prow knelt an old man, his white hair and greenish gray coat making him look like an ancient sea captain. Suddenly he turned to give a quick order to the crew, and the boat came to a stop.

"Captain Christy! He'll get the boy all right." The words of the watching swimmers comforted Nan as she ran up the beach toward the pier from which the boat had started.

"He's been captain of the volunteer life guard for fifty years and can't remember how many lives he's saved. He's taught the boys and girls who come here in the summer to swim and pulled them out when they went in too deep."

Nan could hear no more, for she had reached the end of the tumble-down pier from which Captain Christy had started, and for which the boat was pulling now.

"Don't cry, little lady!" the captain said soothingly as he saw Nan in her black and white bathing suit, and stretching out her arms toward him. "The lad's here, a bit cold but not much the worse for his visit to the fishes."

As he spoke the boat slid alongside the pier and the captain stepped out with Donald in his arms.

"Come up to my house," he said to Nan. "There's a fire going there and that's what the lad needs most now, heat and a hot drink." He strode ahead, and Nan followed to the little weather-beaten shack that had been his only home for over half a century. It looked like the hulk of some old wreck washed up there on the beach, but it was bright with orange nasturtiums that bloomed in the tiny garden and a few flaming red chrysanthemums had opened like the sun setting in red over the sea.

Inside the shack there were a few comforts. The captain laid Donald on the narrow bunk and poked the fire that smoldered in the little sheet-iron stove. Then he set a pot of some thick, savory stuff on it and stirred it as the savory smell began to fill the one tiny room.

Donald lay quietly for a moment. Then he opened his eyes, and color came to his cheeks. All at once he pulled himself up to a sitting position.

"Clam chowder!" he said, looking about him.

"Yes, and you don't deserve it, you rash young scamp," Captain Christy said as he dipped up a brimming tin mug of the chowder and put it into Donald's eager hands. "What made you frighten your little sister so, and send me off on a chase through the surf after you when I was just putting a mess of chowder on to warm for my dinner?" But the Captain's harsh words ended in a chuckle as he gave Donald a resounding slap on his back. "I know what you were up to. You were trying to brave the sea, and that's a fine spirit to have if only you're sure enough of yourself. I must take you in hand and see that you learn how to swim better."

"Oh, thank you, Captain. I'm so much obliged," Donald said, getting on his feet.

"And so will Mother and Father thank you," Nan said. "We're going home in a week, but we'll come over and see you every day. We ought to go now, for someone may have told Mother about Donald, and she will be so frightened."

Captain Christy went to the low door of the shack and looked out over the bare length of the beach and the cottages that would soon be empty.

"Going home!" he repeated. "You'll see lights in the streets at night, and you'll hear clanging bells on cars instead of the lighthouse lamp and the ringing of the bell buoy out in the cold."

"Don't you ever go away from here, not all winter?" Nan asked wistfully.

"I haven't seen a city or kept a holiday in twenty years," Captain Christy said. "The summer folks go, but I stay here and keep warm with driftwood and listen for the cries from the wrecks. I'm as busy in the winter as in the summer, and terribly lonely, little mates."

The last days at the beach flew. Donald and Nan told Captain Christy goodbye, boarded the little steamer that crossed to the mainland, took the train, and the family was at home once more in the city. The beginning of school made them forget the captain waving goodbye to them from the pier. It was nearing Thanksgiving when their father read a newspaper headline aloud at the breakfast table.

"Fishing Boat Wrecked. Saved by Veteran Captain Christy of the Fishers Point Volunteer Guard." Then he laid down the paper. "That man's a hero," he exclaimed. "It's cold as Greenland up at the Point now, and he's close on seventy years old."

"He told us about the winter," Nan said. "The lighthouse lamp is all he can see and the bell buoy all he can hear." She thought a minute. Then she ran over to her father's chair. "I've had a splendid idea!" she said. Then she suggested something to him. "Donald and I were planning it for some time, but wouldn't it be beautiful for Thanksgiving? It could be done, couldn't it, Daddy?"

Her father considered a moment. Then, "Why, yes, it could. We will," he said.

Thanksgiving came in with a northeaster at Fishers Point. The crew of the life boats straggled down to the pier and stamped to keep warm as they looked out over the choppy sea.

"The steamer won't make the trip today," they said. "She hasn't come across in a week now. Over yonder they're eating turkey with their families. Wonder if they ever think of the sailors who haven't seen the mainland since cranberries were planted." Then they fought the wind back to the captain's and sat around the stove, trying to make their own cheer.

Captain Christy put in a few more hunks of wood. As he bent over the wood basket one of the men nudged another.

"See him hold his back," he whispered. "The captain's getting old."

"More lives than he can count, he's brought in," the other whispered back. They started to help the captain, but they were interrupted by three shrill blasts of a whistle that sounded from the direction of the sea. New vigor in his old limbs, the captain sprang to the door, opening it to a blast of wind that cut like a knife.

"It's the boat from the mainland," he shouted. "Maybe she's brought the mail. She's weathered the storm for Thanksgiving, boys!"

Then he got down his glasses. "She's unloading passengers! Who ever heard of that in a gale like this? They've got cargo with them!" At last he voiced the climax. "Shiver my timbers, lads, but the passengers and the cargo are coming this way!"

Donald came first, breathless from his run up the beach, his arms full, and followed by Nan.

"A happy Thanksgiving, Captain," he shouted. "We've come to spend it with you. Father had to pretty nearly buy the steamer to get us over, but here we are."

"And we've brought you a few things to make the winter easier," Nan said.

"And our chauffeur and Father are bringing more things," Donald added.

Tinned meats and vegetables and coffee and milk and tea, blankets, books, and magazines, a roasted turkey, a big cake, jellies— it did not seem possible that their arms could have brought so much comfort and good cheer.

Captain Christy could not speak at first. Then he brushed a suspicious mist from his eyes and reached out his hand to Donald.

"I'm more than grateful," he said huskily. "I know it's all the little mates' doing." Then he turned to his crew.

"Clear the decks, you lazy lubbers!" he laughed. "The ship's going to set sail for Thanksgiving."

They all managed to crowd around the little table that had a piece of sail cloth spread over it for a tablecloth and a bunch of coral in the center to decorate it. A tin pot of coffee on the stove and the warming turkey perfumed the shack.

"Isn't it jolly!" Donald whispered to Nan as he sat on an upturned keg in front of his tin plate.

"Shh!" Nan said. "The captain's going to ask a blessing."

"For strong boats and willing arms and for folks who remember us on the mainland, we give Thee thanks, our Lord of the sea," the Captain said.

Poem for Thanksgiving
by Isaac Watts

Let children hear the mighty deeds
Which God performed of old,
Which in our younger years we saw,
And which our fathers told.

He bids us make his glories known,
His works of power and grace.
And we'll convey his wonders down
Through every rising race.

Our lips shall tell them to our sons,
And they again to theirs;
That generations yet unborn
May teach them to their heirs.

Thus shall they learn in
God alone Their hope securely stands;
That they may ne'er forget his works,
But practice his commands.

There was a moment's hush and then Donald stood up.

"Father says I may give you this," he said, pulling from his pocket a leather box. He snapped it open, and a flashing gold medal was disclosed on a satin cushion. "It's for you for being so brave, and he's arranged for you to come down to us whenever you feel like it, for we've got a room for you in the Sailors' Snug Harbor. It's a beautiful place, just for sailors, with ships going by all the time, and green lawns, and everybody will want to see you and hear you tell stories."

He stopped for breath.

"Three cheers for the captain!" said one of his crew. They all shouted then, and Captain Christy pinned on his medal with shaking fingers.

"Thank you! Thank you!" He said tremulously when they had quieted and begun on the turkey. "That Snug Harbor sounds fine. I'll come to it someday, but this Thanksgiving has put me in trim for a lot of storms yet, thanks to the little mates. That's how it puts heart in an old sailor when the mainland remembers him," he finished gratefully.

Pilgrim Collar and Bonnet

A group of Pilgrims dressed in somber black clothes and white collars gathered around the table and offered a prayer of thanksgiving to God. The image of plainly dressed Pilgrims has become a common image in our country. But did the Pilgrims dress in drab clothing? Not always! The Pilgrims dressed just like other people from England at that time. It was the Puritans who followed a ridged rule for plain dress not the Separatists who we now call the Pilgrims. Then what exactly did the Pilgrims wear? They wore silks, velvet, and broadcloth. They were fond of lace and shoes trimmed with lace. As they adjusted to the New World, their clothing continued to follow what was popular in England.

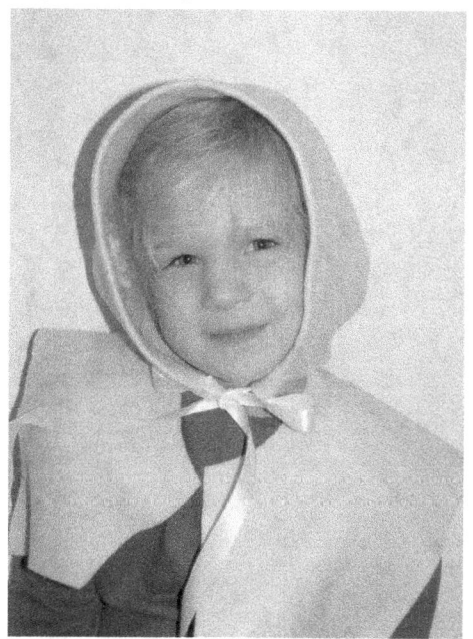

Even though the Pilgrims did not dress in the drab clothing we picture them wearing, the custom has remained and today we will make a girl's Pilgrim bonnet and a Pilgrim collar that may be used for a boy or a girl.

Bonnet

To make a Pilgrim bonnet, take a 20" x 9" piece of white or light colored felt, and fold it lengthwise one inch from the edge. Press with a cool iron. Cut a 60" x 1" ribbon and place it on the inside of the crease. Glue the ribbon to the felt using a glue stick. To wear, place on the head and tie under the chin.

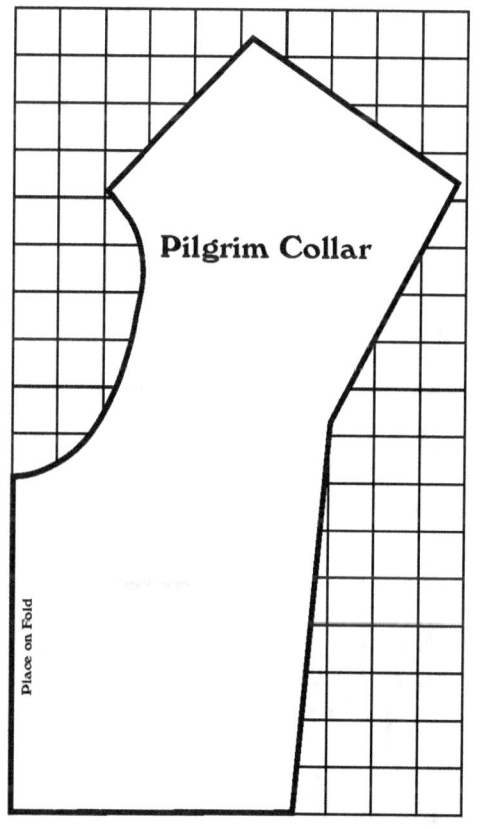

Collar

To make a Pilgrim Collar, use the pattern at right as a guide to cut out a piece of felt. Each square equals one inch. Place the collar over a dark colored shirt or dress and safety pin the front together.

Countdown to Thanksgiving — Amy Puetz

9 Days Until Thanksgiving

The Story of Massasoit

By Robert Mackenzie, 1881

The great benefactor of the Pilgrims at Plymouth was an Indian chief. For more than forty years, when the colony was weak and defenseless, encountering sickness, famine, and peril on every hand, he was its defender and protector. His influence saved it from destruction by the Narragansetts. If any hero deserves a noble monument in New England, it is Massasoit.

This great and good chief dwelt at Sowams, now Warren, Rhode Island. Massasoit's spring is still to be seen near one of the wharves of that town. Another of his favorite residences was Mount Hope, a lovely hill overlooking the Narragansett Bay, where was the principal burying-ground of his people.

Nathaniel Morton in his *New England's Memorial* describes Massasoit as a portly man, grave of countenance and spare of speech. He loved peace and friendship and had a great respect for the wisdom of the Pilgrims.

His tribe and most of the New England tribes had been depleted by a great plague, which had prevailed in New England a few years before the landing of the Pilgrims. We are told that the natives "died in heaps," that their bodies turned yellow after death, and that their unburied bones were often seen in depopulated villages by the first settlers in their explorations. But for this destruction of once powerful tribes, the colonists must have been early overpowered in the Indian wars.

On Thursday, March 22, 1621, one hundred and one days after the landing of the Pilgrims, Massasoit, accompanied by his brother and sixty warriors, came to Plymouth to make a league of friendship with the colony. He had sent word of his coming, but on that day, he suddenly made his appearance on Watson's Hill, which overlooked the settlement, and drew up his braves in a most imposing array. The latter were painted and fantastically dressed. The Pilgrims desired to receive the chief with due honor, but the distressing winter had rendered half their number unfit for such service. But Edward Winslow approached Massasoit with a present and remained with the warriors as a hostage, while the good chief and a body of unarmed men went down the hill to the settlement. Captain Miles Standish, who had mustered a military company of six musketeers, met him.

What a site it was! The Captain gave his orders in deep tones, and the men turned about to face their guest, and saluted. A drum was beaten, and a trumpet sounded; then came Governor Carver to the sachem (chief) and kissed his hand, and the two sat down on a rug and made a treaty of peace which protected the colony for nearly half a century.

Edward Winslow returned the visit of Massasoit during the following summer. In March 1623, news came to Plymouth that the chief was dangerously sick. Mr. Winslow was sent by the colonists to visit him. He was accompanied by Mr. Hamden and by Hobomok, an Indian interpreter.

Hobomok greatly loved his chief. On the way to Sowams in Pokonoket, the residence of Massasoit, he would break out into exclamations of grief, "My loving sachem! Oh, my loving sachem! Many have I known, but never any like thee. Whilst I live I shall never see his like among Indians!"

Mr. Winslow in his journal has left a most interesting account of this visit to Massasoit.

He says, "When we came to the house we found it so full of men that we could scarcely get in, though they used their best endeavors to make way for us. We found the Indians in the midst of their charms for him, making such a noise as greatly affected those of us who were well, and therefore was not likely to benefit him who was sick. About him were six or eight women, who chafed his limbs to keep heat in him.

"When they had made an end of their charming, one told him that his friends, the English, were come to see him. Having understanding left, though his sight was wholly gone, he asked who was come. They told him, Winslow.

"He desired to speak with me. When I came to him, he put forth his hand, and I took it. He then inquired, 'Keen Winslow?' which is to say, 'Art thou Winslow?'

"I answered, 'Ahhe,' that is, 'Yes.'

"Then he said, 'Matta neat wonckanet namen, Winslow;' that is to say, 'Oh Winslow, I shall never see thee again.'

"I then called Hobomok and desired him to tell Massasoit that the Governor, hearing of his sickness, was sorry; and though, by reason of much business, he could not come himself, yet he sent me with such things as he thought most likely to do him good in his extremity, and that if he would like to partake of it I would give it to him. He desired that I would. I then took some conserve (medicine) on the point of my knife and gave it to him, but could scarce get it through his teeth. When it had dissolved in his mouth, he swallowed the juice of it. When those who were about him saw this they rejoiced greatly, saying that he had not swallowed anything for two days before. His mouth was exceedingly furred, and his tongue much swollen. I washed his mouth and scraped his tongue, after which I gave him more of the conserve, which he swallowed with more readiness. He then desired to drink. I dissolved some of the conserve in water and gave it to him.

"Within half an hour there was a visible change in him. Presently his sight began to come. I gave him more and told him of an accident we had met with in breaking a bottle of drink the governor had sent him, assuring him that if he would send any of his men to Patuxet (Plymouth), I would send for more. I also told him that I would send for chickens to make him some broth, and for other things which I knew were good for him, and that I would stay till the messenger returned, if he desired. This he received very kindly, and appointed some who were ready to go by two o'clock in the morning, against which time I made ready a letter.

"He requested that the day following I would take my gun and kill him some fowl, and make him some pottage, such as he had eaten at Plymouth, which I promised to do. His appetite returning before morning, he desired me to make him some broth without fowl before I went out to hunt. I was now quite at a loss what to do. I, however, caused a woman to pound some corn, put it into some water, and place it over the fire. When

Thanksgiving
by F. R. Havergal

Thanks be to God! To whom earth owes
Sunshine and breeze,
The heath-clad hill, the vale's repose,
Streamlet and seas,
The snowdrop and the summer rose,
The many-voiced trees.

Thanks for the darkness that reveals
Night's starry dower;
And for the sable cloud that heals
Each fevered flower,
And for the rushing storm that peals
Our weakness and Thy power.

Thanks for the sweetly-lingering might
In music's tone;
For paths of knowledge, whose calm light
Is all thine own;
For thoughts that at the Infinite
Fold their bright wings alone.

Yet thanks that silence oft may flow
In dew-like store:
Thanks for the mysteries that show
How small our lore;
Thanks that we here so little know
And trust Thee all the more

Thanks for the gladness that entwines
Our path below;
Each sunrise that incarnadines
The cold still snow;
Thanks for the light of love which shines
With brightest earthly glow.

Thanks for Thine own thrice-blessed Word,
And Sabbath rest;
Thanks for the hope of glory stored
In mansions blest;
Thanks for the Spirit's comfort poured
Into the trembling breast.

Thanks, more thanks, to Him ascend,
Who died to win,
Our life, and every trophy rend
From Death and Sin;
Till, when the thanks of earth shall end,
The thanks of Heaven begin.

we went out to seek herbs, but it being early in the season, we could find none except strawberry leaves. I gathered a handful of them, with some sassafras root, and put them into the porridge. It being boiled; I strained it through my handkerchief, and gave him at least a pint, which he liked very well. After this his sight mended more and more, and he took some rest. We now felt constrained to thank God for giving his blessing to such raw and ignorant means. It now appeared evident that he would recover, and all of them acknowledged us as the instruments of his preservation.

"That morning he caused me to spend in going from one to another of those who were sick in town, requesting me to wash their mouths also, and to give to each of them some of the same that I gave him. This pains I willingly took.

"The messengers who had been sent to Plymouth had by this time returned, but Massasoit, finding himself so much better, would not have the chickens killed, but kept them that they might produce more. Many, whilst we were there, came to see him; some of them, according to their account, came not less than a hundred miles. Upon his recovery, he said, '"Now I see that the English are my friends, and love me, and whilst I live I will never forget this kindness which they have shown me.'

"As we were about to come away he called Hobomok to him and revealed to him a plot the Massachusetts had formed to destroy the English. He told him that several other tribes were confederate with them; that he, in his sickness, had been earnestly solicited to join them, but had refused, and that he had not suffered any of his people to unite with them."

Massasoit died, as is supposed, in the autumn of 1661, forty-one years after the landing of the Pilgrims. In 1662, his two sons, Wamsetta and Metacom, came to Plymouth to renew the treaty of peace he had made and desired that English names should be given them. The court named them after the two heroes of Macedon, Alexander and Philip.

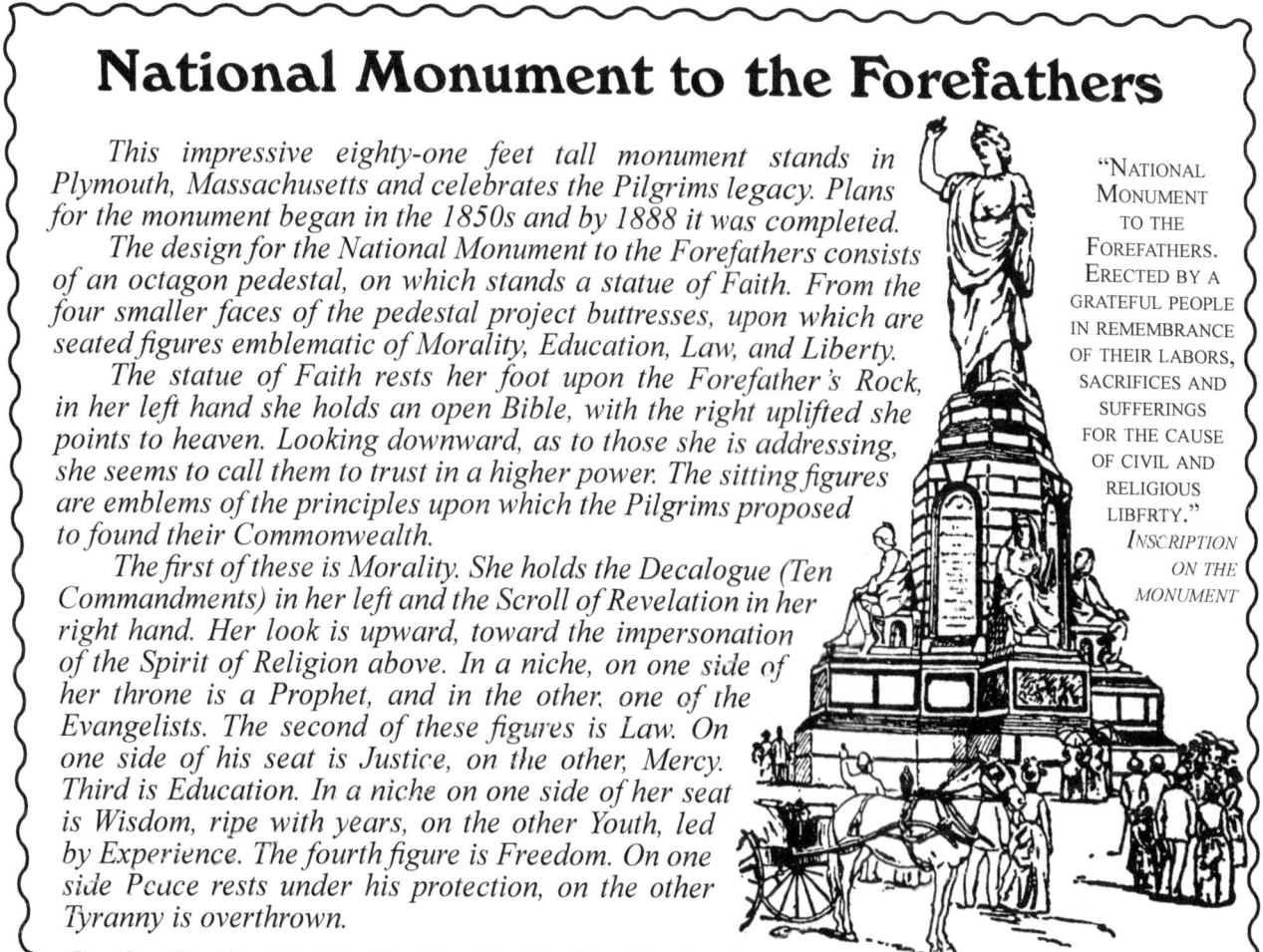

National Monument to the Forefathers

This impressive eighty-one feet tall monument stands in Plymouth, Massachusetts and celebrates the Pilgrims legacy. Plans for the monument began in the 1850s and by 1888 it was completed.

The design for the National Monument to the Forefathers consists of an octagon pedestal, on which stands a statue of Faith. From the four smaller faces of the pedestal project buttresses, upon which are seated figures emblematic of Morality, Education, Law, and Liberty.

The statue of Faith rests her foot upon the Forefather's Rock, in her left hand she holds an open Bible, with the right uplifted she points to heaven. Looking downward, as to those she is addressing, she seems to call them to trust in a higher power. The sitting figures are emblems of the principles upon which the Pilgrims proposed to found their Commonwealth.

The first of these is Morality. She holds the Decalogue (Ten Commandments) in her left and the Scroll of Revelation in her right hand. Her look is upward, toward the impersonation of the Spirit of Religion above. In a niche, on one side of her throne is a Prophet, and in the other, one of the Evangelists. The second of these figures is Law. On one side of his seat is Justice, on the other, Mercy. Third is Education. In a niche on one side of her seat is Wisdom, ripe with years, on the other Youth, led by Experience. The fourth figure is Freedom. On one side Peace rests under his protection, on the other Tyranny is overthrown.

"NATIONAL MONUMENT TO THE FOREFATHERS. ERECTED BY A GRATEFUL PEOPLE IN REMEMBRANCE OF THEIR LABORS, SACRIFICES AND SUFFERINGS FOR THE CAUSE OF CIVIL AND RELIGIOUS LIBERTY."
INSCRIPTION ON THE MONUMENT

Hat and Headdress

Indian Headdress

The Pilgrims had a very good relationship with their neighbors, the Wampanoags. This friendship lasted for nearly fifty years.

Today we are going to make a simple Indian headdress. To do this cut two strips of construction paper 1¼" x 12" and staple them together, so they make a band that goes around the head. Tape feathers to the inside of the band. The feathers were usually worn on the back of the head.

Pilgrim Hat

To make a Pilgrim hat, you will need black poster board, a paper plate (I used a 10½ plate, but if you have a bigger one that will work too).

Cut the poster board 22" long and 7" high. Also cut two other strips of poster board, one 22" long by 2" high, and another one 22" long by 1" high.

Tape the 22" x 7" piece of poster board together so it makes a tube. This will be the hat tube. Place the hat tube in the center of the plate and trace it (FIG. 1).

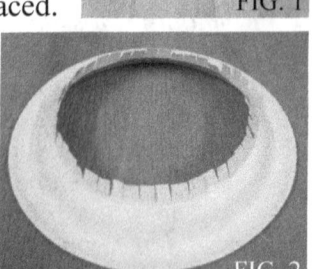

FIG. 1

Cut a circle in the plate half and inch on the inside of the line you traced. Next, cut slits from the inside of the circle to the traced line. Fold these sections up (FIG. 2).

Place the hat tube on the plate and use double stick tape (or glue) to connect the plate to the hat tube (FIG. 3).

Paint the plate using black craft paint.

Once it is dry glue or tape the 2" x 22" poster board around the outside of the hat tube. This will cover up any paint that might have ended up on the poster board.

FIG. 2

Make a copy of the buckle below and use it as a pattern to cut out the buckle using yellow or gold paper.

Tape or glue the 22" x 1" poster board to the inside of the hat to cover up part of the plate that is connected to the hat tube.

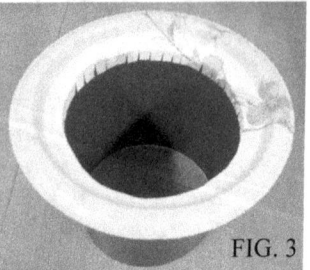

FIG. 3

If you want to make a top for the hat, just make a circle a little larger than the hat band and cut little slits and fold them down and glue or tape them to the hat tube. I chose not to do this, to simplify the process.

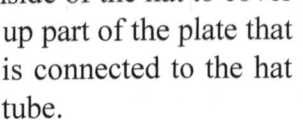

Buckle, cut along dotted lines

8 Days Until Thanksgiving

The Mother of Thanksgiving

By Amy Puetz

We know the story of the Pilgrims inviting the Indians to join them for a special celebration of Thanksgiving to God. What is perhaps not known is how Thanksgiving became a national holiday. It's one of those exciting little sidelines of history! How did Thanksgiving become a national holiday? It came about in a most unusual way, as you shall see.

For many years, Thanksgiving was celebrated by only a few states, mostly in the New England area. The date varied—some would celebrate it after the harvest, others when the cattle were brought home from their summer pastures. In 1795, John Jay, who was serving as the Governor of New York, attempted to set a uniform day for his state to celebrate Thanksgiving, but the cities preferred to keep their own customs and his plan failed. In some places, Thanksgiving lost its status and slowly fell into oblivion. The person who saved Thanksgiving was a kind, Christian lady named Sarah Josepha Buell Hale.

Sarah was born on October 24, in 1788 to Revolutionary War veteran Captain Gordon Buell. Sarah's education took place at home under the direction of her mother, Martha, and brother, Horatio. After completing her schooling, she taught for several years. In 1813, she married David Hale and after nine short years of marital bliss, he died. The widow had four small children with a fifth on the way.

What could she do? Sarah Hale decided to make a living using her pen. This Christian woman took that unassuming weapon, called *the pen,* and for nearly fifty years she used it to shape the ideals of the United States. Her driving force was her desire to raise her children and provide a good education for them. In 1828, she became the editor of the *Ladies Magazine.* Fearlessly she packed up her belongings and five children and moved from her village home in Newport, New Hampshire, to the bustling city of Boston.

The magazine changed hands in 1836 when Louis Antoine Godey of Philadelphia bought it and changed the name to *Godey's Lady's Book.* Sarah Hale did not move to Philadelphia right away. Her youngest son, William, was attending Harvard and until he graduated she felt she must provide a home for him in Boston. In 1841, she set out for the city of "Brotherly Love" and there she served as the editor of the most popular woman's magazine until 1877.

Sarah Hale's move to Philadelphia made her aware that the lovely holiday of Thanksgiving was completely ignored in Pennsylvania. Perhaps someone should help make it a national holiday? Thus, began a campaign that would last nearly twenty years. This idea was not completely new to the industrious lady. In her novel, *Northwood,* published in 1827, one of her characters said, "We have too few holidays. Thanksgiving, like the Fourth of July, should be considered a national festival, and observed by all our people. . . . We want it as the exponent of our Republican institutions, which are based on the acknowledgment that God is our Lord, and that, as a nation, we derive our privileges and blessings from Him."

In 1846, Sarah began her official campaign in *Godey's Lady's Book*. Now she had a means of reaching thousands of people with her dream of making Thanksgiving a national holiday. Not only did she make eloquent appeals in the magazine, but she also wrote many letters. In her clever and persuasive tone, she petitioned governors, congressmen, and even presidents. She personally sent a plea to every president, from Zachary Taylor to Abraham Lincoln. Each year she gained a few more supporters.

In 1852, she boasted in the *Lady's Book* that, "Last year, twenty-nine states, and all the territories, united in the festival. This year, we trust that Virginia and Vermont will come into this arrangement, and that the governors of each and all the states and territories will appoint Thursday, the 25th of November, as the Day of Thanksgiving." To Sarah, the significance of Thanksgiving surpassed the modern notion of pumpkin pie, turkey, and overeating. She believed Thanksgiving would help promote patriotism and unite the country. In 1852, she said, "Families may be separated so widely that personal reunion

Excerpt from Godey's Lady's Book Magazine
by Sarah Josepha Hale

Thanksgiving Day for 1854—For several years past we have discussed the subject of a general agreement on the time of this annual autumnal festival. We believe the people would be gratified to have this union of sentiment carried into effect. The last Thursday in November has been selected as the day best suited to the general convenience, when the people from Maine to Mexico, from the Atlantic to the Pacific, might sit down together, as it were, and enjoy in national union their feast of gladness, rendering thanks to Almighty God for the blessings of the year.

Therefore we pray, on behalf of all friends of the "Lady's Book," that the governors of the several states and territories would issue their proclamations, each one for his own state, unanimously appointing Thursday, the 30th of November, as the Day of Thanksgiving! Will not the press throughout the Union join the "Lady's Book" in this petition?

would be impossible; still this festival, like the Fourth of July, will bring every American heart into harmony with his home and his country. The influence of such an American festival on foreigners would also be salutary, by showing them that our people acknowledge the Lord as our God. In our own wide land . . . every heart would, on one day in each year, beat in unison of enjoyment and thankfulness. Therefore, we hope to witness this year the first of these national festivals." She encouraged her readers to contact their leaders to ask them to support a national Thanksgiving celebration.

Why is Thanksgiving celebrated on the fourth Thursday in November? This also is a bit of little-known history with an interesting story. The actual date of the Pilgrims' first Thanksgiving was unrecorded and open to debate. Sarah Hale chose the date set by George Washington. In 1789, Elias Boudinot presented the idea of having a National Day of Thanksgiving and Prayer. President George Washington set November 26 (the fourth Thursday of the month) as the special day for that purpose. His proclamation sounds more like a sermon than a political announcement. It said, "to recommend to the people of the United States a day of public thanksgiving and prayer, to be observed by acknowledging with grateful hearts the many and signal favors of Almighty God, especially by affording them an opportunity peaceably to establish a form of government for their safety and happiness. . . . To the service of that great and glorious Being who is the beneficent Author of all the good that was, that is, or that will be; that we may then all unite in rendering unto him our sincere and humble thanks for his kind care and protection of the people of this country previous to their becoming a nation." At the time of this proclamation, Sarah was one-year-old. Later she would labor to keep the spirit of Washington's proclamation alive for future generations.

Her dream of a national day of Thanksgiving happened during an unlikely time. Even the dark days of the Civil War did not stop her from writing to President Lincoln, requesting that he make Thanksgiving a national holiday. Abraham Lincoln agreed with the persuasive editor; Thanksgiving should be celebrated throughout the country. On October 3, 1863, he signed a proclamation setting the last Thursday of November aside as a day of Thanksgiving. A portion of the proclamation stated, "The year that is drawing towards its close has been filled with the blessings of fruitful fields and healthful skies. To these bounties, which are so constantly enjoyed that we are prone to forget the source from which they come, others have been added, which are of so extraordinary a nature, that they cannot fail to penetrate and soften even the heart which is habitually insensible to the ever watchful providence of Almighty God."

Every president after Lincoln issued a Thanksgiving proclamation, and for over fifty years the tradition remained untouched. In the 1930s, the date of Thanksgiving was in danger of being altered. President Franklin Roosevelt wanted to extend the holiday shopping season in 1939 by moving Thanksgiving to the third Thursday in November. The hope was that it would boost the economy, but it didn't. People were upset that the traditional date was changed, and the holiday was mockingly called, "Franksgiving."

Some states celebrated on the third Thursday, others celebrated on the traditional date and two states, Colorado and Texas, celebrated on both dates. Afterwards, congress passed a resolution making the fourth Thursday the official date of Thanksgiving!

Without the help of Sarah Hale, Thanksgiving probably would have fallen into obscurity, as other holidays have done. She saw it as a day of spending time with family and praising God for his many blessings. It's exciting to see what one person with a big heart and perseverance can do! When you celebrate Thanksgiving this year, by all means talk about the Pilgrims and their amazing legacy, but also remember the remarkable lady named Sarah Hale, who was the Mother of Thanksgiving!

Our National Thanksgiving Day
By Sarah Hale, 1868

This article appeared in a book Sarah Hale wrote in 1868 called Manners. *In it she tells why the United States needs Thanksgiving. Older children and adults will enjoy this article the most. ~ Amy*

"Then he said unto them, Go your way, eat the fat, and drink the sweet, and send portions unto them for whom nothing is prepared; for this day is holy unto our Lord: neither be ye sorry; for the joy of the Lord is your strength." Nehemiah 8:10

Such was the order given to the people of Israel, for the celebration of one of their religious festivals. We learn from this that a day of yearly rejoicing and giving of gifts was not only sanctioned but enjoined by divine authority on God's chosen people. Such yearly festival is not positively enjoined on Christians; but that it is both expedient and beneficial may safely be argued, when we find that the practice was approved by our God and Father in heaven.

Our day of thanksgiving represents, in many striking coincidences, the Jewish feasts. Only make our day national, and we should then represent the union of joy that was the grand proof of the Divine blessing. Such social rejoicings tend greatly to expand the generous feelings of our nature, and strengthen the bond of union that binds us brothers and sisters in that true sympathy of American patriotism which makes the Atlantic and Pacific Oceans mingle in our mind as waters that wash the shores of kindred homes, and mark from east to west the boundaries of our dominion.

One of the coincidences to which we have alluded is the custom of giving gifts, and "sending portions to those for whom nothing is prepared." I venture to assert that there is not a public institution of any sort, charitable or reformatory, hospital or prison, which is not remembered at this time by a plentiful dinner, liberally provided by our citizens.

The Creator has so constituted humans that their minds need a moderate portion of amusement as imperatively as the body at times wants stimulating food. This re-creative joyousness, this return, if you please, to the happiness of childhood, is good for the soul. It sweetens the temper, it brightens hope, increases our love for each other, and our faith in the goodness of God. There are individuals and nations who, from an unhappy state of things, never "drink the sweet nor eat the fat," but drag on a miserable and starved existence.

God intended that all our faculties should, in the right way, be exercised, and neglect of such exercise changes us to incomplete creatures. Our busy, wealth seeking people require to have days of national festivity, when fashion and custom will call them to the feast of love and thanksgiving.

The editress of the *Lady's Book* has for the past twenty years been in the habit of urging upon the attention of its readers and friends, year by year, the plan of a National Thanksgiving Day.

We suggested the last Thursday in November, as the most suitable day to set apart by the governor of each state for this festival, which would then become a national jubilee. This time was selected because then the agricultural labors of the year are generally completed, the elections over, those autumnal diseases which usually prevail more or less have ceased, and the summer wanderers are gathered to their homes. We have received letters approving this Union festival from governors of nearly every state and territory who had, before the war commenced, approved the idea although all had not acted upon it.

Thanksgiving day has been an establishment of custom, not a law; without state legislation, there cannot always be unity among the governors. In 1862, all the states which observed the day, united upon the last Thursday in November, except Massachusetts and Maine: these two held their Thanksgiving the first Thursday in December, because it was the anniversary of the separation of Maine from the parent state.

Is it not a better plan to have, in the first instance, the day appointed by a proclamation from the President of the United States? As head of the nation, as well as the chief of the army and navy, the authority rests with him, and by his action on this point perfect certainty of unity of observance would be secured.

The way is already prepared: the last Thursday in November has been observed as the American festival day for the last five or six years, not only on our own shores, but by Americans in European cities, and wherever our countrymen could meet together—on board our fleets in the Mediterranean, African, and Brazilian stations; by our missionaries in India, China, Africa; and in 1860, it was observed by our countrymen in Japan, and also in Constantinople, Berlin, Paris, and other places.

Our late beloved and lamented President Lincoln recognized the truth of these ideas as soon as they were presented to him. His reply to our appeal was a proclamation, appointing the last Thursday in November, 1863, as the day of national thanksgiving. President Johnson's Proclamation for the National Thanksgiving on the last Thursday of November, 1866, was observed over all the country. Thus the family union of states and territories in our Great Republic was fixed and hallowed by the people in the ninetieth year of American Independence.

No one can doubt the effect upon us, as a nation, of acknowledging God, at least once in a year, and returning thanks to Him publicly for the infinite mercies so lavishly bestowed upon us. Nor only upon ourselves is this influence. Such an observance by us will not be unfelt by the nations of the Old World. There is something peculiarly beautiful in seeing a great people, of the most varying creeds and opinions, bound by no established faith, thus voluntarily uniting throughout our wide land to mingle their voices in one common hymn of praise and thanksgiving. Thus, and thus only, can we show to the world that America is indeed a Christian Republic.

Everything that contributes to bind us in one vast empire together, to quicken the sympathy that makes us feel, from the icy North to the sunny South, that we are one family, each a member of a great and free nation, not merely the unit of a remote locality, is worthy of being cherished. We have sought to re-awaken and increase this sympathy, believing that the fine filaments of the affections are stronger than laws to keep the union of our states sacred in the hearts of our people.

We believe that our Thanksgiving Day, if thus fixed and perpetuated, will be a great and sanctifying promoter of this national spirit. Our whole people will then look forward to it—make preparations to honor and enjoy it.

I have thus endeavored to lay before my readers one of the strongest wishes of my heart, convinced that the general estimate of feminine character throughout the United States will be far from finding it an objection that this idea of American Union Thanksgiving was suggested by a woman. The enjoyments are social, and the feastings are domestic; therefore this annual festival is really the exponent of family happiness and household piety, which women should always seek to cultivate in their hearts and in their homes. God gave to man authority, to woman influence: she inspires and persuades; he convinces and compels.

It has always been my aim to use my influence in this womanly way. And now I feel, that, under the blessing of God, I am indebted to the efficient aid of good and patriotic men, who have accomplished this idea of establishing the last Thursday in November as the set time for the people of the United States, wherever they may chance to be, to celebrate and hallow as the American National Thanksgiving Day.

Recipes

Among Sarah Hale's other accomplishments, she also published several cookbooks. In these books she had several recipes for what she called, "real Yankee pie" or pumpkin pie. The recipe at right is from 1852 and shows how vague recipes from this era were. Below is a modern recipe from the Puetz family kitchen.

Pumpkin Pie (Modern Recipe)

3 eggs
1 cup sugar
1 tsp. salt
½ tsp. cinnamon
½ tsp. ginger
¼ tsp. cloves
1 cup scalded milk
2 cups pumpkin

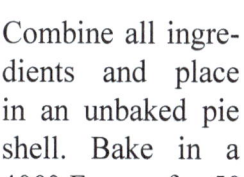

Combine all ingredients and place in an unbaked pie shell. Bake in a 400° F oven for 50 minutes or until a knife inserted near the center comes out clean.

How to Roast a Turkey

Remove the plastic piece between the legs of the turkey and sprinkle salt in the cavity. Separate the skin from the turkey on the breast and insert 2 Tbsp. of butter, 2 slices of onion, and several celery leaves on each side. The butter, onion, and celery should be held in place by the skin. These will give the meat extra flavor. Place the turkey in a roasting pan, cover with foil, and seal all around. Place in a 325° F preheated oven. Check package for directions on the amount of time to bake. About half way through baking, loosen the foil and baste the turkey every half hour until done, replacing the foil as best as possible without getting burned. The turkey is done when a leg can be easily moved and broken away from the rest of the turkey. Turkey roasted in a roasting oven instead of a range oven seems to be more moist.

The Ladies' New Book of Cookery

By Sarah Hale

Pumpkin Pie (1852 Recipe)

Take out the seeds, and pare the pumpkin or squash; but in taking out the seeds do not scrape the inside of the pumpkin; the part nearest the seed is the sweetest. Then stew the pumpkin, and strain it through a sieve or cullender. To a quart of milk, for a family pie, 3 eggs are sufficient. Stir in the stewed pumpkin with your milk and beaten-up eggs, till it is as thick as you can stir round rapidly and easily. If the pie is wanted richer make it thinner, and add sweet cream or another egg or two; but even 1 egg to a quart of milk makes very decent pies. Sweeten with molasses or sugar; add 2 teaspoonsfuls of salt, 2 tablespoonsfuls of sifted cinnamon, and 1 tablespoonsful of powdered ginger; but allspice may be used, or any other spice that may be preferred. The peel of a lemon grated in gives it a pleasant flavor. The more eggs, says an American authority, the better the pie. Some put 1 egg to a gill (½ cup) of milk. Bake about an hour in deep plates, or shallow dishes, without an upper crust, in a hot oven.

Recipes

Pumpkin Log

¾ cup sifted all-purpose flour
1 tsp. baking powder
2 tsp. ground cinnamon
1 tsp. pumpkin pie spice
½ tsp. ground nutmeg
½ tsp. salt
3 eggs slightly beaten
1 cup sugar
⅔ cup canned solid pack pumpkin
1 cup chopped walnuts

Preheat oven to 375° F. Line a 15"x10" jelly roll pan with wax paper. Grease and flour the wax paper. Set aside.

Combine flour baking powder, cinnamon, pumpkin pie spice, nutmeg, and salt in a bowl. In a separate large bowl beat eggs and sugar well with a wire whip until light and fluffy. Beat in pumpkin. Stir in dry ingredients until moistened. Pour into the pan with wax paper and spread as evenly as possible. Sprinkle the nuts over the top as evenly as possible. Bake 15 minutes in a 375° oven, until the center of the cake springs back when touched.

Remove from the oven. Moisten a clean dish towel slightly and lay out smoothly on the counter, and cover with wax paper, then sprinkle the wax paper with confectioner sugar. Carefully flip the pan over onto the towel and wax paper and remove pan from the cake. Loosen the wax paper from the edges of the cake, using a knife if necessary. Slowly peal the wax paper from the entire cake, again using a knife if necessary to separate the wax paper from the cake. Trim ¼ inch from the edges if they are too dry and overcooked.

Roll up cake, towel, and wax paper together starting from the short side. Place on a wire rack to cool completely. This usually takes about 2 hours.

Unroll when cooled and spread with cream cheese filling. Gently reroll cake and refrigerate until ready to serve.

This cake freezes nicely to be used at a later time. Simply wrap with plastic wrap and then with freezer paper or foil if desired.

Cream Cheese Filling

1 package 8 oz. Cream cheese, softened
6 Tbsp. butter, softened
1 cup confectioner sugar
1 tsp. vanilla

Beat ingredients together until smooth.

7 Days Until Thanksgiving

The Thanksgiving Goose

By Fannie Wilder Brown, 1908

But I don't like roast goose," said Guy, pouting. "I'd rather have turkey. Turkey is best for Thanksgiving, anyway. Goose is for Christmas."

Guy's mother did not answer. He watched her while she carefully wrote G. T. W. on the corner of a pretty new red-bordered handkerchief. Five others, all alike, and all marked alike lay beside it. The initials were his own.

"Why didn't you buy some blue ones? I'd rather have them different," he said.

Mrs. Wright smiled a weary little smile but did not answer. She lighted a large lamp and held the marked corner of one of the handkerchiefs against the hot chimney. The heat made the indelible ink turn dark, although the writing had been so faint Guy hardly could see it before.

"Oh, dear," he cried, "there's a little blot at the top of that T! I don't want to carry a handkerchief that has a blot on it."

"Very well," said his mother. "I'll put them away, and you may carry your old ones until you ask me to let you carry this one. I don't care to furnish new things for a boy who doesn't appreciate them."

"I don't like old—"

"That'll do, Guy. Never mind the rest of the things that you don't like. I want you to take this dollar down to Mrs. Burns. Tell her that I shall have a day's work for her on Friday, and I thought she might like to have part of the pay in advance to help make Thanksgiving with. Please go now."

"But a dollar won't help much. She won't like that. She always acts just as if she was as happy as anybody. I don't want to go there on such an errand as that."

Mrs. Wright smiled again, but her tone was very grave.

"Mrs. Burns is 'as happy as anybody,' Guy, and she has the best-behaved children in the neighborhood. The little ones almost never cry, and I never have seen the older ones quarrel. But there are eight children, and Mr. Burns has only one arm, so he can't earn much money. Mrs. Burns has to turn her hands to all sorts of things to keep the children clothed and fed. She'll be thankful to get the dollar—you see if she isn't! And tell her if she is making mince pies to sell this year, I'll take three."

Guy walked very slowly down the street until he came to the little house where the Burns family lived.

"I'd hate to live here," he thought. "I don't see where they all sleep. My room isn't big enough, but I don't believe there's a room in this house as big as mine. I shouldn't have a bit of fun, ever, if I lived here. And I'd hate to have my mother make pies and send me about to sell them."

Then he knocked on the front door, for there was no bell. No one came. He could hear people talking in the distance, so he knew some of the family were at home. Someone always was at home here to look after the little children. He walked around to the kitchen door. It stood open. The children were talking so fast they did not hear his knock.

They were very busy. Katie, the eleven-year-old, and Malcolm, ten, Guy's age, were cutting citron into long, thin strips, piling it on a big blue plate. Mary and James, the eight-year-old twins, were paring apples with a paring machine. The long, curling skins fell in a large stone jar standing on a clean paper, spread on the floor. Charlie, who was only four years old, was watching to see that none of the parings fell over the edge of the jar. Susan, who was seven, was putting raisins, a few at a time, into a meat chopper screwed down on the kitchen table. George, three years old, was turning the handle of the chopper to grind the raisins. Baby Joe was creeping about the kitchen floor after a kitten. Mrs. Burns was taking a great piece of meat from a steaming kettle on the back of the stove. Everyone was working, except the baby and the kitten, but all seemed to be having a glorious time. What they were saying seemed so funny it was some time before Guy could understand it. At last he was sure it was some kind of a game.

"Mice?" asked Susan. Mary squealed, and they all laughed.

"Because they're small," said Mary. "Snakes?"

"They can't climb trees," Mrs. Burns called out from the pantry. The children fairly roared at that. "A pantry with no window in it?"

"Oh, we've had that before," Katie answered. "I know what you say. It's a good place to ripen pears in when Mrs. Wright gives us some."

Guy knocked very loudly at that. He had not thought that he was listening.

The children started, but did not leave their work. They looked at their mother. "Jamie," she said. Then Jamie came to meet Guy, and invited him to walk in.

"What game is it?" asked Guy, forgetting his errand.

"Making mince pies," said Jamie. "It's lots of fun. Don't you want to play? I'll let you turn the paring machine if you'd like that best."

Guy said, "thank you" and began to turn the parer eagerly.

"But I don't mean what you are doing," said Guy. "I knew that was mince pies. I thought that was work. I meant what you were saying. It sounds so funny! I never heard it before."

"Mamma made it up," explained Malcolm. "It's great fun. We always play it at Thanksgiving time. You think of something that people don't like, and the one who can think first tells what he is thankful for about it. We call it 'Thanksgiving.'"

Guy stayed for an hour and played Thanksgiving while helping with the mince pies. Then, quite to his surprise, the twelve o'clock whistles blew, and he had to go home. But he remembered his errands and did them, to the great pleasure of the whole Burns family.

In the afternoon Guy spent some time writing a note to his mother. It was badly written, but it made his mother happy. It read:

Dear Mother,

I am Thankful the blot isn't any bigger. I am Thankful the handkerchiefs isn't black on the borders. I would like that one with the Blot on to put in my pocket when you read this. But my old ones are nice. The Burns family don't have things to be Thankful for but they are Thankful just the same.

I am Thankful for the Goose we are going to have. The best is I am Thankful I am not a Goose myself, for if I was I wouldn't know enough to be Thankful.

Respectfully yours,
Guy Theodore Wright

Thanksgiving the Game

Play the game Thanksgiving that is mentioned in this story. What are some things that you don't really like? Can you think of something to be thankful about those things? Have fun!

6 Days Until Thanksgiving

A Mystery in the Kitchen

By Olive Thorne Miller, 1905

Something very mysterious was going on in the Jarvis kitchen. The table was covered with all sorts of good things—eggs and butter and raisins and citron and spices; and Jessie, with her sleeves rolled up and a white apron on, was bustling about, measuring and weighing and chopping and beating and mixing those various ingredients in a most bewildering way.

Moreover, though she was evidently working for dear life, her face was full of smiles; in fact, she seemed to have trouble to keep from laughing outright, while Betty, the cook, who was washing potatoes at the sink, fairly giggled with glee every few minutes, as if the sight of Miss Jessie working in the kitchen was the most amusing thing in the world.

It was one of the pleasantest sights that big, sunny kitchen had seen for many a day, and the only thing that appeared mysterious about it was that the two workers acted strangely like conspirators. If they laughed—as they did on the slightest provocation—it was very soft and at once smothered. Jessie went often to the door leading into the hall, and listened; and if there came a knock on the floor, she snatched off her apron, hastily wiped her hands, rolled down her sleeves, asked Betty if there was any flour on her, and then hurried away into another part of the house, trying to look cool and quiet, as if she had not been doing anything.

On returning from one of these excursions, as she rolled up her sleeves again, she said, "Betty, we must open the other window even if it is cold. Mamma thought she smelled roast turkey!"

Betty burst into a laugh which she smothered in her apron. Jessie covered her mouth and laughed, too, but the window was opened to make a draught and carry out the delicious odors, which, it must be confessed, did fill that kitchen so full that no wonder they crept through the cracks, and the keyholes, and hung about Jessie's dress as she went through the hall.

"What did ye tell her?" asked Betty, as soon as she could speak.

"Oh, I told her I thought potpie smelled a good deal like turkey," said Jessie, and again both laughed. "Wasn't it fortunate we had potpie today? I don't know what I should have said if we hadn't."

Well, it was not long after that when Jessie lined a baking-dish with nice-looking crust, filled it with tempting looking chicken legs and wings and breasts and backs and a bowlful of broth, laid a white blanket of crust over all, tucked it in snugly around the edge, cut some holes in the top, and shoved it into the oven just after Betty drew out a dripping pan in which reposed, in all the glory of rich brown skin, a beautiful turkey. Mrs. Jarvis couldn't have had any nose at all if she didn't smell that. It filled the kitchen full of nice smells, and Betty hurried it into the pantry, where the window was open to cool.

Then Jessie returned to the spices and fruits she had been working over so long, and a few minutes later she poured a rich, dark mass into a tin pudding-dish, tied the cover on tight, and slipped it into a large kettle of boiling water on the stove.

"There!" she said, "I hope that'll be good."

"I know it will," said Betty confidently. "That's y'r ma's best recipe."

"Yes, but I never made it before," said Jessie doubtfully.

"Oh, I know it'll be all right, 'n' I'll watch it close," said Betty; "'n' now you go'n sit with y'r ma. I want that table to git dinner."

"But I'm going to wash all these things," said Jessie.

"You go long! I'd ruther do that myself. 'Twon't take me no time," said Betty.

Jessie hesitated. "But you have enough to do, Betty."

"I tell you I want to do it," Betty insisted.

"Oh, I know!" said Jessie, "you like to help about it. Well, you may; and I'm much obliged to you, besides." And after a last look at the fine turkey cooling his heels (if he had any) in the pantry, Jessie went into the other part of the house.

When dinner time arrived and Papa came from town, there duly appeared on the table the potpie before mentioned, and various other things pleasant to eat, but nothing was seen of the turkey so carefully roasted nor of the chicken pie, nor of the pudding that caused the young cook so much anxiety. Nothing was said about them, either, and it was not Thanksgiving nor Christmas, though it was only a few days before the former.

It was certainly odd, and stranger things happened that night. In the first place, Jessie sat up in her room and wrote a letter; and then, after her mother was in bed and everything still, she stole down the back stairs with a candle, quietly, as though she was doing some mischief. Betty, who came down to help her, brought a box in from the woodshed; and the two plotters, very silently, with many listenings at the door to see if any one was stirring, packed that box full of good things.

In it the turkey, wrapped in a snowy napkin, found a bed, the chicken pie and the plum pudding—beautiful looking as Betty said it would be—bore him company; and numerous small things, jam jars, fruits, etc., filled the box to its very top. Then the cover, provided with screws so that no hammering need be done, was fastened on.

"Now you go to bed, Miss Jessie," whispered Betty. "I'll wait."

"No, you must be tired," said Jessie.

"But I'd ruther," said Betty shortly, "'n' I'm going to. It won't be long now."

So Jessie crept quietly upstairs, and before long there was a low rap on the kitchen door. Betty opened it, and there stood a man.

"Ready?" said he.

"Yes," answered Betty; "but don't speak loud; Miss Jarvis has sharp ears, 'n' we don't want her disturbed. Here's the card to mark it by," and she produced a card from the table.

The man put it in his pocket, shouldered the box, and Betty shut the door.

Not one of those good things ever went into the Jarvis dining room!

The next morning things went on just as usual in the house. The kitchen door was left open and Mrs. Jarvis was welcome to smell any of the appetizing odors that wafted out into her room. Jessie resumed her study, and especially her practice, for she hoped some day to be a great musician. She waited on her mother and took charge of the housekeeping, so much as was necessary with the well-tried servant at the head of the kitchen. And though she had but sixteen years over her bright brown head, she proved herself to be what in that little New England town was called "capable."

But that box of goodies! Let us see where it went.

It was Thanksgiving morning in a rough-looking little mining settlement in Colorado. In a shanty rougher and more comfortless than the rest were two persons. One, a man of thirty, was deeply engaged in cleaning and oiling a gun which lay in pieces about him on the rough bench where he sat; the other, a youth of sixteen, was trying to make a fire burn in the primitive-looking affair that did duty as a stove. Both wore coarse miner's suits, and picks and other things about the room told that their business was to dig for the yellow dust we are all so greedy to have.

Evidently their efforts had been fruitless, for the whole place appeared run down, and the two looked absolutely hungry.

It was Thanksgiving morning, as I said, but no thankfulness shone in the two pale, thin faces. Both were sad, and the younger one almost hopeless.

"Jack," said the elder, pausing in his operations, "mind you give that old hen a good boil, or we won't be able to eat it."

"It'll be better'n nothing, anyway, I suppose," said Jack gloomily.

"Not much. 'Specially if you don't get the taste of sage brush out of it. Thankfully, I happened to get that shot at her, anyway," he went on, "I've seen worse dinners—even Thanksgiving dinners—than a sage hen."

"I haven't," said Jack shortly; for the mention of Thanksgiving had brought up before him with startling vividness the picture of a bright dining room in a certain town far away, a table loaded with good things, and surrounded by smiling faces, and the contrast was almost more than he could bear.

"Well, don't be down boy, so long as you can get a good fat hen to eat, if she does happen to be too fond of seasoning before she's dead!" replied the other cheerfully. "We haven't struck it yet, but it's always darkest just before dawn, you know. We may be millionaires before this time tomorrow."

"We may," answered Jack; but he didn't look as if he had much hope of it.

A few hours later the occupants of the cabin sat down to their Thanksgiving dinner. It consisted of the hen aforesaid, cut in pieces and boiled—looking very odd, too—served in the kettle in which the operation had been performed. The table was at one end of the bench, the table service two jackknives and two iron spoons—absolutely nothing else.

The elder sat on the bench, the younger drew up a keg that had held powder, and the dinner was about to begin.

But that hen was destined never to be eaten, for just at that moment the door was pushed open in the rude way of the country, a box set down on the floor, and a rough voice announced, "A box for Mr. Jack Jones."

Jack started up.

"For me, there must be a mistake! Nobody knows—" he stopped, for he had not mentioned that his name was assumed.

"Likely not!" said the man, with a knowing look, "but folks has a mighty strange way of findin' out," and he shut the door and left.

Jack stood staring at the box as if he had lost his wits. It could not be from home, for no one knew where he went when he stole out of the house one night six months ago and ran away to seek his fortune. Not a line had he ever written—not even when very ill, as he had been; not even when without a roof to cover his head, as he had been more than once; not even when he had not eaten for two days, as also, alas, had been his experience.

He had deliberately run away, because—how trivial it looked to him now, and how childish seemed his conduct—because he thought his father too hard on him; would not allow him enough liberty; wanted to dictate to this man of sixteen; he intended to show him that he could get on alone.

Poor Jack, the only comfort he had been able to extract from his hard lot these many months of wandering, of work, of suffering such as he had never dreamed of—his only comfort was that his tender mother didn't know, his only sister would no more be worried by his grumbling and complaints, and his father would be convinced now that he wasn't a baby. Small comfort, too, to balance the hardships that had fallen to his lot since the money he had drawn from the savings bank was used up.

"Why don't you open it?" The gruff but not unkind voice of his roommate, whom he called Tom, aroused him. "Maybe there's something in it better'n sage hen," trying to raise a smile.

But no smile followed. Mechanically Jack sought the tools to open it, and in a few moments the cover was off.

It was from home! On the very top was a letter addressed to Jack Jarvis in a hand that he well knew.

He hastily stuffed it into his pocket unopened. The layers of paper were removed, and as each one was thrown off, something new appeared. Not a word was spoken, but the kettle of sage hen was silently put on the floor by Tom as the bench began to fill up. A jar of cranberry sauce, another of orange marmalade, oranges and apples, a plum pudding, a chicken pie, and lastly, in its white linen wrapper, the turkey we saw browning in that far-off New England kitchen.

As one by one these things were lifted out and placed on the bench a deep silence reigned in the cabin. Jack had choked at sight of the letter, and memories of days far different from these checked even Tom's usually lively tongue. A strange unpacking it was; how different from the joyful packing at dead of night with those two laughing girl faces bending over it!

When all was done, and the silence grew painful, Jack blurted out, "Help yourself," and bustled about, busily gathering up the papers and folding them, and stuffing them back in the box, as though he were the most particular housekeeper in the world. But if Jack couldn't eat, something, too, ailed Tom. He said simply, "Don't feel hungry. Believe I'll go out and see what I can find," and shouldering his gun, now cleaned and put together, he quickly went out and shut the door.

Jack sat down on the keg and looked at the things which so vividly brought home, and his happy life there, before him. He did not feel hungry, either. He sat and stared for some time. Then he remembered his letter. He drew it from his pocket and opened it. It was rather thin, and when he pulled it out of the envelope the first thing he saw was the smiling face of his sister Jessie, his twin sister, his playmate and comrade, his confidante from the cradle. The loss of her ever-willing sympathy had been almost more to him than all the rest of his troubles.

This was another shock that brought something to his eyes that made him see the others through a mist. There were the pictures of his mother, whose gentle voice he could almost hear, and of his father, whose gray hairs and sad face he suddenly remembered were partly his work.

At last he read the letter. It began:

Dear Jack,
    I've just found out where you are, and I'm so glad. I send you this Thanksgiving dinner. It was too bad for you to go off so. You don't know how dreadful it was for Mamma; she was sick a long time, and we were scared to death about her, but she's better now; she can sit up most all day.

    Oh, Jack! Father cried! I'm sure he did, and he almost ran out of the room, and didn't say anything to anybody all day. But I was determined I'd find you. I shan't tell you how I did it, but Uncle John helped me, and now, Jack, he says he wants just such a fellow as you to learn his business, and he'll make you a very good offer. And, Jack, that's my turkey—my Winnie—and nobody but Betty knows anything about this box and this letter.

    I send you all my money out of the savings bank (I didn't tell anybody that), and I want you to come home. You'll find the money under the cranberries. I thought it would be safe there, and I knew you'd eat them all, you're so fond of cranberries. I didn't tell anybody because I want to surprise them, and besides, let them think you came home because you got ready. It's nobody's business where you got the money anyway. Now do come right home, Jack. You can get here in a week's time, I know.

                                      Your affectionate sister,
                                       Jessie

Jack laid the letter down with a rush of new feelings and thoughts that overwhelmed him. He sat there for hours; he knew nothing of time. He had mechanically turned the cranberry jar upside down and taken from the bottom, carefully wrapped in white paper, fifty dollars.

A pang went through him. Well did he know what that money represented to his sister; by how many sacrifices she had been saving it for a year or two, with the single purpose of taking the lessons from a great master that were to fit her to teach, to take an independent position in the world, to relieve her father, who had lost a large slice of his comfortable income, and who was growing old and sad under his burden. She had often talked it over with Jack.

Now she had generously given up the whole to him, all her hopes and dreams of independence; and he—he who should have been the support of his sister, the right arm of his father—he had basely deserted.

These thoughts and many more surged through his mind that long afternoon, and when Tom returned as the shadows were growing long, he sat exactly as he had been left.

On Tom's entrance he roused himself. There was a new light in his eye.

"Come, Tom," he said, "dinner's waiting. You must be hungry by this time."

"I am that," said Tom, who had been through his own mental struggles meanwhile.

The two sat down once more to their Thanksgiving dinner, and this time they managed to eat, though Jack choked whenever he thought of tasting a bit of Jessie's pet turkey, Winnie; and much as he liked turkey, and a home turkey at that, he could not touch it.

After the meal, when the provisions were stored away in the cupboard (a soap box) much too small for such a supply, it had grown quite dark, and the two, still disinclined to talk, went to their beds—if the rough bunks they occupied may be dignified by that name.

But not to sleep—at least not Jack, who tumbled and tossed all night and got up in the morning with an energy and life he had not shown for weeks.

After breakfast Tom shouldered his pick and said, "I'll go on, Jack, while you clear up." Yet he felt in his heart he should never see Jack again. For there was a homestruck look in his face that the man of experience in the ways of runaway boys knew well.

He was not surprised that Jack did not join him, nor that when he returned at night to the cabin he found him gone and a note pinned up on the door, "I can't stand it—I'm off for home. You may have my share of everything, Jack."

It was a cold evening in early December, and there seemed to be an undercurrent of excitement in the Jarvis household. The table was spread in the dining room with the best silver and linen. Mrs. Jarvis was better, and had even been able to go into the kitchen to superintend the preparations for dinner.

Jessie went around with a shining face that no one understood and she could not explain.

Betty was strangely nervous, and had made several blunders that morning which mortified the faithful servant very much. An air of expectancy pervaded the whole house, though the two heads of it had not a hint of the cause.

Jessie heard the train she had decided to be the important one. She could hardly contain herself for expectation. She tried hard to calm herself now and then by the thought, "Perhaps he won't come," but she couldn't stay serious, for she felt as certain that he would as that she lived.

You all know how it happened. The door opened and Jack walked in. One instant of blank silence, and then a grand convulsion.

Jack fell on his knees with his face in his mother's lap, though he had not thought a moment before of doing any such thing. Jessie hung over him, frantically hugging him. Mr. Jarvis, vainly trying to join this group, could only lay his hands on Jack's head and say in a broken voice, "My son! My son!" While Betty performed a war dance around the party, wildly brandishing a basting spoon in one hand and wiping her streaming eyes on the dishcloth which she held in the other.

It was long before a word could be spoken, and the dinner was totally ruined, as Betty declared with tears (though they were not for sorrow), before any one could calm down enough to eat.

Then the reaction set in, and justice was done to the dinner, while talk went on in a stream. Jack did not tell his adventures; he only said that he had come from the city, where he had made arrangements for a situation with Uncle John—at which Jessie's eyes sparkled. His looks, even after a week of comfort and hope, spoke for his sufferings.

There is little more to tell. Jack Jarvis at seventeen was a different boy from the Jack who at sixteen started out to seek his fortune. You may be sure that Jessie had her music lessons after all, and that a new Winnie with a fine young brood at her heels stalked about the Jarvis grounds the next spring.

Thanksgiving Song

Sing the song below and discuss what it means.

We Gather Together

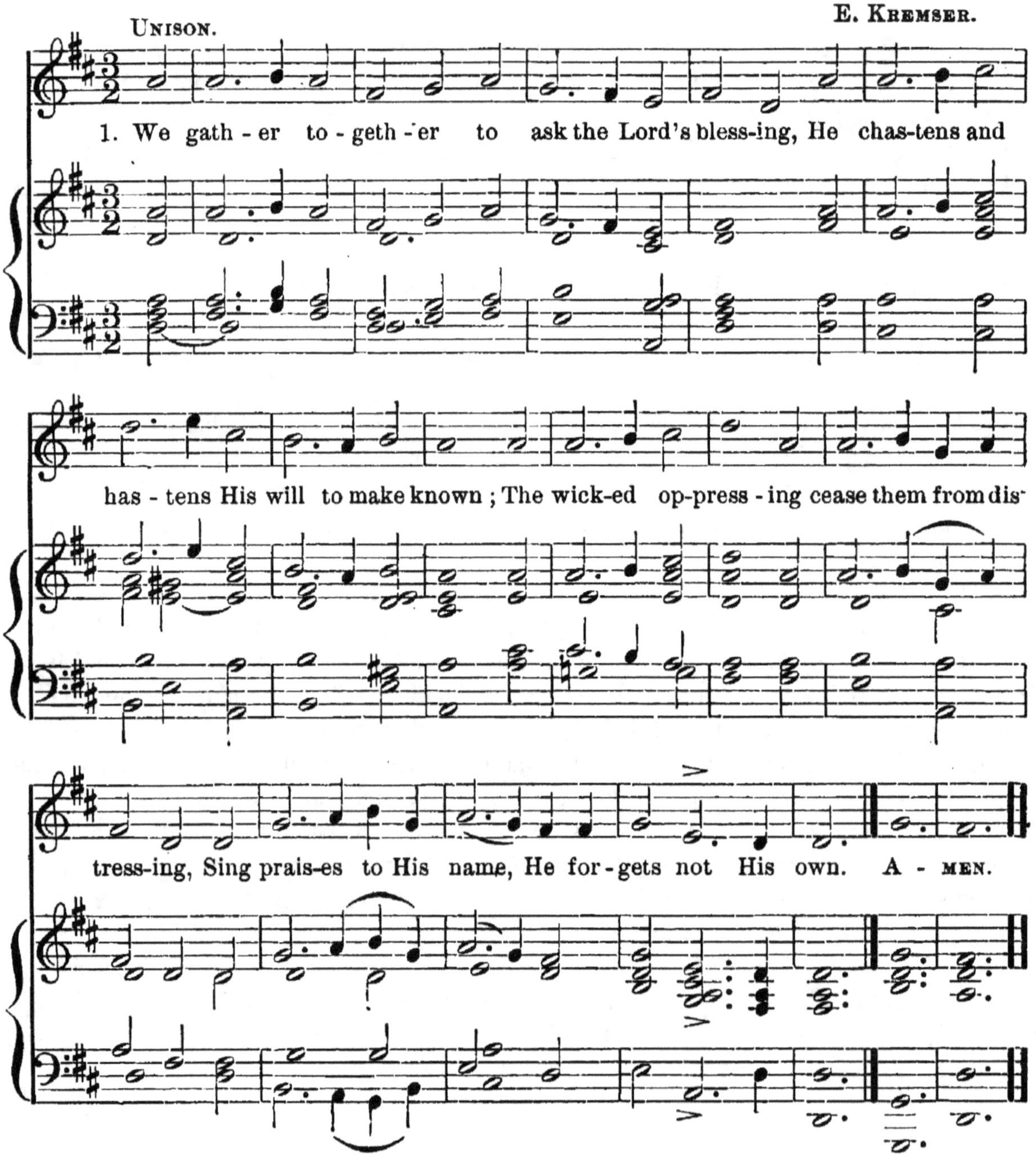
Unison.
E. Kremser.
1. We gath - er to - geth - er to ask the Lord's bless-ing, He chas-tens and
has - tens His will to make known; The wick-ed op-press - ing cease them from dis-
tress-ing, Sing prais-es to His name, He for - gets not His own. A - men.

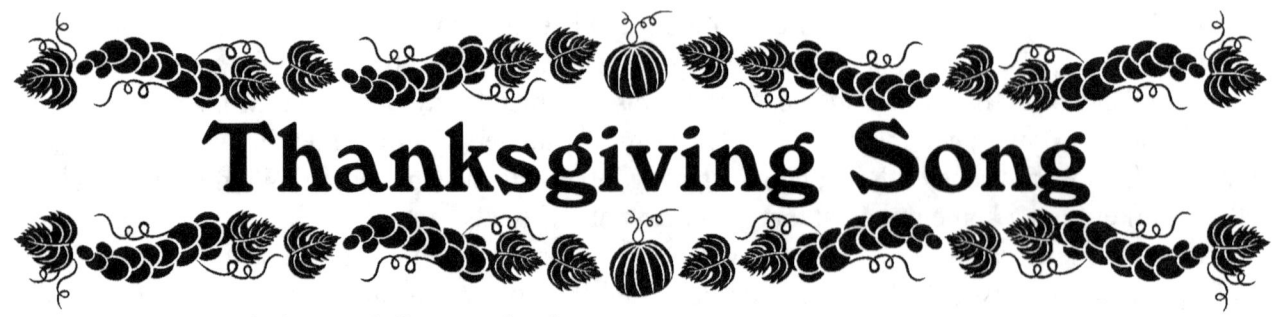

Countdown to Thanksgiving

5 Days Until Thanksgiving

Why He Carried the Turkey

By James Baldwin, 1912

In Richmond, Virginia, one Saturday morning, an old man went into the market to buy something. He was dressed plainly, his coat was worn, and his hat was dingy. On his arm he carried a small basket.

"I wish to get a fowl for tomorrow's dinner," he said.

The market man showed him a fat turkey, plump and white and ready for roasting.

"Ah! that is just what I want," said the old man. "My wife will be delighted with it."

He asked the price and paid for it. The market man wrapped a paper round it and put it in the basket.

Just then a young man stepped up. "I will take one of those turkeys," he said. He was dressed in fine style and carried a small cane.

"Shall I wrap it up for you?" asked the market man.

"Yes, here is your money," answered the young gentleman, "and send it to my house at once."

"I cannot do that," said the market man. "My errand boy is sick today, and there is no one else to send. Besides, it is not our custom to deliver goods."

"Then how am I to get it home?" asked the young gentleman.

"I suppose you will have to carry it yourself," said the market man. "It is not heavy."

"Carry it myself! Who do you think I am? Fancy me carrying a turkey along the street!" said the young gentleman; and he began to grow very angry.

The old man who had bought the first turkey was standing quite near. He had heard all that was said.

"Excuse me, sir," he said, "but may I ask where you live?"

"I live at Number 39, Blank Street," answered the young gentleman, "and my name is Johnson."

"Well, that is fortunate," said the old man, smiling. "I happen to be going that way, and I will carry your turkey, if you will allow me."

"Oh, certainly!" said Mr. Johnson. "Here it is. You may follow me."

When they reached Mr. Johnson's house, the old man politely handed him the turkey and turned to go.

"Here, my friend, what shall I pay you?" said the young gentleman.

"Oh, nothing, sir, nothing," answered the old man. "It was no trouble to me, and you are welcome."

He bowed and went on. Young Mr. Johnson looked after him and wondered. Then he turned and walked briskly back to the market.

"Who is that polite old gentleman who carried my turkey for me?" he asked of the market man.

"That is John Marshall, Chief Justice of the United States. He is one of the greatest men in our country," was the answer.

The young gentleman was surprised and ashamed.

"Why did he offer to carry my turkey?" he asked.

"He wished to teach you a lesson," answered the market man.

"What sort of lesson?"

"He wished to teach you that no man should feel himself too fine to carry his own packages."

"Oh, no!" said another man who had seen and heard it all. "Judge Marshall carried the turkey simply because he wished to be kind and obliging. That is his way."

All Good Gifts Around Us
by Matthias Claudius, 1782
translated by Jane Montgomery Campbell

We plough the fields, and scatter the good seed on the land;
But it is fed and watered by God's almighty hand:
He sends the snow in winter, the warmth to swell the grain,
The breezes and the sunshine, and soft refreshing rain.
All good gifts around us
Are sent from heaven above,
Then thank the Lord, O thank the Lord
For all His love.

Thanksgiving Skit

Thanksgiving is just around the corner. How would you like to preform a play for your family on Thanksgiving day? You could use one of the stories in this book to create your own play, or you could use the one below. If you begin practicing now, you should have plenty of time to be ready for Thanksgiving. If you do not have a large number of actors, you might combine several characters into one. The three female characters in scene two could be played by one person. Several of the male characters could also be combined into one character. You may dress up in Pilgrim costumes, or you may wear modern dress and just say the lines. Either way, have fun and imagine what it would have been like to have lived in Plymouth during the first Thanksgiving.

Scene 1
A home in Plymouth

Characters

Governor Bradford   Elder Brewster

(Elder Brewster goes to Governor Bradford's house. He knocks.)
Governor Bradford: Good morrow!
Elder Brewster: Come in and sit down.
Governor Bradford: Thank you, I will. (They sit down.) How well the crops have turned out. All that we planted has grown finely. Everybody has plenty of corn and wheat now, for the winter.
Elder Brewster: Yes, I have come to see you about having a Thanksgiving Day. We ought to thank God. It is He who made the corn and wheat to grow. Don't you think we ought to set apart a day for Thanksgiving?
Governor Bradford: Yes, I do. It is hardly a year since we came over in the *Mayflower*. What hard times we had at first! We were cold and hungry, and afraid of the Indians. How much better off we are now! Our houses are built. The Indians are friendly. And our storehouses are full of corn. We ought, indeed, to thank God.
Elder Brewster: Let us have a Thanksgiving feast!
Governor Bradford: And let us invite the Indians to it!
Elder Brewster: Yes, do. I will tell everybody in Plymouth to get ready. And you send the invitation to the Indians. We'll have a great Thanksgiving feast.

Scene 2
In the kitchen of a Plymouth home on Thanksgiving day.

Characters

Stephen Hopkins   Mrs. White
John Alden   Captain Standish
Priscilla Mullins   Mary Chilton
Governor Bradford   Elder Brewster
Massasoit   Samoset
Squanto

(Stephen comes running into Plymouth. All the other Pilgrims gather around him.)
Mrs. White: What's the news?
Stephen: I took the invitation to the Indians, and they are coming.
John: How shall we talk to them? They speak a different language.
Priscilla: That's so. What shall we do? We cannot understand them.
Stephen: Oh! That will be all right. Squanto can translate for us.
Mrs. White: Come now, let us get the dinner ready. Who will help?
Stephen: I will. I'll go to the beach and dig clams. (He takes a pail and shovel and goes to the beach.)
John: I'll go fishing. (He takes a fishing rod and goes fishing in the bay.)
Captain Standish: I'll go to the woods and shoot wild turkeys. (He takes his gun and goes to the woods.)
Priscilla: I'll make a corn-meal pudding. (She stirs in a bowl.)
Mary: I'll give you a hand, Priscilla. With all this baking we will need extra wood in the fireplace. (She puts wood on the fire.)
Governor Bradford: I'll put the tables and chairs in their places. We'll eat out here under the trees.
Mrs. White: I'll set the tables.
Stephen: (He comes back.) Here, Mary. I have dug a pail of clams.
Mary: Good! I'll cook them.
John: (He comes back.) Here, Priscilla. I have caught some fish.
Priscilla: That's good. I'll broil them.
Captain Standish: (He comes back.) See here, Mrs. White. I have shot some turkeys.
Mrs. White: Oh, what big ones! I'll dress them and roast them right away.
Captain Standish: Hark! Here come the Indians. (In march the Indians.)
Governor Bradford: Welcome, Massasoit. Welcome, Samoset. Welcome, Squanto. (He bows graciously.) You are all welcome to our Thanksgiving dinner.
Elder Brewster: Please gather together everyone (all come near). We are here to give thanks to God for His many blessings over the last year. Although we have faced many trials, God has been faithful. Today, we remember His gracious gifts, and we give thanks. Let us recite Psalm 100.
Everyone:

Make ye a joyful noise unto
Jehovah, all the earth:
Serve ye Jehovah with gladness
Before Him come with mirth
Know, that Jehovah He is God,
Not we ourselves but He
And not ourselves: his own people
And sheep of his pasture are we.
Enter into his gates with praise,
Into his Courts with thankfulness
Make ye confession unto him,
And His name reverently bless.
Because Jehovah He is good,
His bountiful mercy
is everlasting and His truth
is to eternity.

4 Days Until Thanksgiving

Helen's Thanksgiving

By Susan Coolidge, 1883

"Mamma, would you mind *very* much if I should learn to make pies?" This request sounds harmless, but Mrs. Sands quite started in her chair as she heard it. She and Helen were sitting on either side of a wood-fire. The blinds had been pulled down to exclude the chilly November darkness, and the room was lit only by the blazing logs, which sent out quick, bright flashes followed by sudden soft shadows, in that unexpected way which is one of the charms of wood-fires. It was a pretty room, in a pretty house, in one of the up-town streets of New York, and the mother and daughter looked very comfortable as they sat there together.

"Pies, my dear? What do you mean?"

"I'll tell you, Mamma. You're going to Grandmamma Ellis for Thanksgiving, this year, and Papa and I are going up to Vermont, to Grandmother Sands?"

"Yes."

"Well, I don't remember Grandmother much, because it is so long since she was here, but the one thing I do recollect is how troubled she was because I didn't know anything about housekeeping. One day you had a headache, and wanted some tea; and you rang and rang, and Jane was ever so long in fetching it, and at last Grandmother said, 'Why don't you run down and see to it, Helen?' And when I told her that I wasn't allowed to go into the kitchen, and beside that I didn't know how to make tea, she looked so distressed, and said, 'Dear me, dear me! Poor little ignorant girl! What a sad bringing up for you in a country like ours!' I didn't understand exactly what she meant, but I have never forgotten it, and do you know, Mamma, just that one speech of hers has made me want to do ever so many things. I never told you, but once I made my bed each morning for a week, until Bridget said I was 'worth my salt as a chambermaid,' and I used to dust the nursery, and sweep. And the other day it came into my head suddenly how pleased Grandmother would be if I carried her a pumpkin pie that I had made myself; so I asked Morrison, and she said she'd teach me if you didn't mind. Do you mind, Mamma?"

"You know, dear, I don't like to have you about with the servants, and I never wanted you to become a servant at home, as so many American girls are. Then you have your lessons to attend to besides."

"Yes, Mamma, I know, but it will only take one morning, and I'll not begin until school closes, if you'd rather not. I really would like to so much, Mamsie?"

Helen's pet name for her mother was coaxingly spoken and had its effect. Mrs. Sands yielded.

"Very well, Dear, you may, if you like, only I wish you could wear gloves."

"Oh Mamma! Nobody makes pies in gloves. But I needn't put my hands in at all, except for rolling the paste, Morrison says so."

Mrs. Sands was not so silly a woman as she sounds. Born in the West Indies, the constant talk about servants and housekeeping, that met her ears when she came to New York, a young married woman, so puzzled and annoyed her that she somewhat rashly decided that her child should never know anything about such matters. Morrison, the good old cook, had lived with her since Helen was a baby, and all had gone so smoothly that there had never seemed occasion for interference from anybody. And Helen would have grown up in utter ignorance of all practical matters, had not a chance remark of her thrifty New England grandmother piqued her into the voluntary wish of learning.

It was with a good deal of excitement, and a little sense of victory as well, that Helen went downstairs, a few days later, to take the promised lesson. The kitchen looked very cheerful and neat, and Morrison was all ready with a big calico apron to tie over Helen's dress. The pie-making lesson was a complete success. By Morrison's advice, she wrote the whole process down in a book while it was fresh in her mind, and she was glad afterwards that she had done so, as you will see.

That same afternoon Mrs. Sands went on to Philadelphia, and next morning early Helen and her father started for their journey to Vermont. It was gray, blustering weather, but neither of them cared for that. Papa was in high spirits, and full of fun as a schoolboy. Their baggage comprised, besides two suitcases, a big hamper full of all sorts of nice things for Grandmother, game and fruit and groceries, and Helen carried a flat basket in her hand, in which, wrapped in a snowy napkin, reposed one of the precious pies.

"Bless me, how blustery it is! It looks as though it were going to snow," said Mr. Sands, as he came in from a walk up and down the platform of one of the little stations at which the train stopped.

Not five minutes later Helen, with a little scream of surprise, cried out, "Why, Papa, it is snowing!" Sure enough it was, in fine snowflakes, which before long thickened.

"It will only be a squall," Mr. Sands said, but the conductor shook his head, and remarked that up there so near the mountains there was no calculating on weather. It might stop in half an hour, or it might go on all night. No one could pretend to say beforehand which it would do.

By the time they reached Asham, their stopping-place, the ground was solid white. The wind, too, had risen, and was drifting the snow in all directions. The hotel manager at Asham, to whom Mr. Sands went for a team, advised them to stay all night, but this both Helen and her father agreed was not to be thought of. It was only fourteen miles. Grandmother was expecting them and must not be disappointed. So, well wrapped in carriage blankets and buffalo robes, they set out in a light covered rockaway, with a stout horse, their baggage packed in behind them.

Fourteen miles may seem a very short distance or a very long one, according to circumstances. Before they had gone halfway both of them began to think it an extremely long one. The road went uphill for the greater part of the way. Night was coming on fast, and every moment the drifts grew thicker and more confusing. Mr. Sands in his secret heart repented that he had not taken the hotel manager's advice, and stayed at Asham. At last the horse, which had halted several times and been urged on again, came to a dead stop. Mr. Sands touched him with the whip, but he would not stir. He jumped up to see what was the matter, and found the poor animal up to his chest in snow. He had wandered from the road a little and plunged into a drift. Mr. Sands tried to turn them toward the road, when, lo, a loud and ominous crack was heard, and Helen gave a scream. One of the shafts had snapped in two.

Matters now looked serious. Mr. Sands undid the harness as fast as possible, for he feared the horse might flounder to release himself, and upset the carriage. Then he climbed into the rockaway again, and stood up to see if he could anywhere see the light of a house. A twinkling beam was visible farther up the hill, about a quarter of a mile away.

"Helen," he said, "I'll have to ask you to sit here quietly for ten minutes or so, while I ride on to a house which I see up there, and get someone to help us. Will you be afraid to be left alone? It's only for a little while."

"N-o; but Papa! Must you go? I'm so afraid the horse will kick, or you'll tumble off."

"Never fear," he tried to laugh, "I really must go, Helen. It's our only chance of getting out of this scrape. Promise me to sit perfectly until, and on no account to leave the carriage."

It seemed much longer than ten minutes before Papa got back, but there he was at last, with another man carrying a lantern, both of them white with snow up to their waists.

"All right, Helen," he cried cheerily. "Wrap all the blankets round your shoulders; I'm going to set you on the horse, and Mr. Simmons and I—this is Mr. Simmons, my dear—will walk on either side and hold you on; we'll have you up the hill in a jiffy."

Helen did not like it at all. The horse felt dreadfully alive under her, and jerked so, as he plunged uphill through the snow, that she was constantly afraid of tumbling off. It did not last long, however. In five minutes her father had lifted and carried her in, and set her down in a kitchen, where a woman with a candle in her hand stood waiting for them.

"This is Mrs. Simmons," he said. "She is so kind as to say that she will keep us until tomorrow morning, when perhaps the snow will have stopped, and, at all events, we shall have daylight to find our way. Mr. Simmons and I are going back now to fetch up the luggage. The rockaway will have to take care of itself until tomorrow, I fancy."

Left alone, Helen looked curiously about her. The kitchen was a bare-looking place to her eyes. There was a stove with a fire in it, a rocking chair covered with a faded patch, some wooden chairs, a table, and a sort of dresser with dishes. A large wheel for spinning wool stood in one of the windows.

Everything was clean, but there was an air of poverty, and to Helen it seemed a most dismal place. She could not imagine how people could live and be happy there.

Mrs. Simmons herself looked very ill and tired. "I enjoy such poor health," she explained to Helen, as she took some plates and bowls down from the dresser. "I got the ague (fever) down to Mill Hollow, where we lived, and we moved up here, hoping to get rid of it. I am some better, but it took me powerful hard yesterday, and I suppose I'll have it bad again tomorrow. Mr. Simmons, he's got behindhand somehow, and it's hard work trying to catch up in these times. What with one thing and another, both of us have felt clean discouraged this fall. Gloria, fetch the milk."

"Yes, Mother." And out of the cellar came a girl of about Helen's age, with a pan in her hands. She had apparently tumbled out of bed to help in the entertainment of the strangers, for her hair was flying loose, and she wore an old nightgown but she had pretty brown eyes and a bright smile.

"I feel real bad to think I'm out of tea," said Mrs. Simmons. "Father, he was calculating to get some later on, when he'd finished a job of lumber-hauling. And the hens have almost stopped laying, too; I hain't but four eggs in the house."

"Oh, don't give us the eggs!" cried Helen, "you'll want them yourself for Thanksgiving, I'm sure."

"Thanksgiving! Dear me, so it is!" said Mrs. Simmons. "I'd forgot all about that. Not that it'd have made much difference, anyway. You can't make something out of nothin', and that's about what we've come to."

"I've got a pie," cried Helen, with a sudden generous impulse, but feeling a little pang meanwhile, as she recalled her vision of putting the pie into Grandmother's own hands. But where was the pie? She recollected now—the basket was in her lap when Papa lifted her out of the carriage. It must have fallen out, and probably was now buried in snow.

A great stamping of boots just then announced the entrance of the two men with the suitcases and hamper. Mrs. Simmons renewed her apologies about the tea. Hot milk, a little fried pork, two of the eggs, and a loaf of soda bread were all she had to offer, but it was very welcome to the hungry travelers. There was some choice tea in Grandmother's hamper, but Mr. Sands very rightly judged it better to say nothing about it just then, as it might have seemed that he and Helen were not satisfied with their supper. They ate heartily, and soon after went to bed in two chilly little lofts upstairs, where all the buffalo robes and blankets from the carriage could not quite keep them warm.

Helen lay awake a long time, thinking of her own disappointment and Grandmother's, but more about the Simmons family. How hard and melancholy their life seemed, struggling with poverty and ague up here among the lonely hills, with no doctor near them, and no neighbors! A great sympathy and pity awoke in her heart. Her first impulse, when she roused next morning, was to hurry to the window. It was still snowing, and the drifts seemed deeper than ever!"

Oh, dear!" she thought, "we shall have to stay in this forlorn place another day, I am afraid." A more generous thought followed. "If it seems so hard to me to have to spend one day here, what must it be to live here always?" And she made up her mind that, if they were forced to stay, she would do all she could to make Thanksgiving a little less forlorn than it seemed likely to be to Mrs. Simmons and Gloria.

It did look forlorn downstairs in the bare little kitchen. Mrs. Simmons's chill was coming on. She was up and dragging herself about, but she looked quite unfit to be out of bed. Two little children, a boy and a girl, whom Helen had not seen the night before, clung close to her dress, and followed wherever she moved, hiding their shy faces from the strangers. They got over their shyness gradually as Helen laughed, and coaxed them, and by the time breakfast was over had grown good friends.

"Now," said Helen, happily, after a last glance at the window, which showed the snowstorm still raging, "I am going to propose a plan. You shall go to bed, Mrs. Simmons—I'm sure you ought to be there at this moment, and Gloria and I will wash the dishes, and we will cook the Thanksgiving dinner."

"Oh, dear! There ain't nothing worth cooking," sighed poor Mrs. Simmons, but she was too ill to make objections. So Gloria, put the kitchen to rights with Helen's help, and then the two girls sat down to consult about dinner.

"Could you roast a turkey, do you think?" asked Helen.

"There ain't no turkey to be roasted," objected Gloria.

"Yes, but could you if there were? Because I think there's one in the hamper. Papa and I know Grandmother would let us have it if she knew."

"Why, of course she would. Use everything in the hamper if you like; Grandmother would never think of objecting, and there's plenty more to be had where those came from," said her father.

So the hamper was unpacked, and the turkey extracted, and a package of tea and another of lump sugar, and a jar of currant jelly; and Helen filled a big dish with oranges and white grapes, and the preparations went merrily on. There proved to be half a squash in the cellar, and Gloria, wading out in the snow, fetched in a couple more eggs from the barn, so pies were possible. Helen produced her recipe book.

"Now I'm going to show you just how to make pies," she said. "I only learned myself day before yesterday." And she thought, "How fortunate it is that I did learn, for now I can show Gloria, and she'll always know. But wouldn't Morrison open her eyes if she could see me?"

The ingredients came out of the hamper, of course, and the crust had to be made of salt butter and no lard; but the pies turned out very good, for all that, and no one was in the least disposed to find fault with their flavor. Really, the little dinner was a great success. Gloria's potatoes were a little underdone, but that was the only failure. The children ate as though they could never be satisfied. Mr. Simmons cheered up and cracked one or two feeble jokes; and even Mrs. Simmons, propped high in bed to survey the festive scene, called out that it "looked something like," and she didn't know when there had been so much laughing going on in their house before.

The clock struck three just as the last nicely washed plate was set away on the dresser. Helen quite jumped at the sound. How short, after all, the day had seemed which promised to be so long and dismal! And just then a bright yellow ray streamed through the window, and, looking out, she saw blue sky.

"Papa," she screamed, "it has cleared up! I do believe we shall get to Grandmother's tonight, after all!"

And so they did. Mr. Sands, with Mr. Simmons's assistance, fitted the rockaway on to a pair of old sledge-runners, and, with many warm goodbyes from the whole family, they drove off. Just at sunset they reached Morrow Hill, and Grandmother was so glad to see them, and they so glad to get there, that it was easy to forget all their disappointment and delay. In fact, after a little while Helen convinced herself that the whole thing was rather a pleasant experience than otherwise.

"For, don't you see, Papa," she exclaimed, "we had all Thanksgiving evening with Grandmother, you know, and she had it with us, so we only lost part of our pleasant time? But if it hadn't been for the snow and the breakdown, the poor Simmons family wouldn't have had any Thanksgiving at all—not a bit; so it really was a great deal better, don't you see that it was, Papa?"

Thanksgiving Proclamation

Before Thanksgiving became a national holiday presidents and governors would issue a day of thanksgiving to be celebrated. Today we are going to write our own proclamation for a day of thanksgiving. The proclamations by Washington and Lincoln are given as samples. It would be simple to follow their format In the beginning they say how they are thankful to God, then they go on to list the ways God has blessed them. After reading the proclamations of Washington and Lincoln, write your own using the questions below. A blank page with an antique looking edge is provided for you to write or print your proclamation. You may copy it on colored paper or you may color it yourself.

How has God blessed you?

Are there things you need to ask God to forgive?

Why should we take some time to give thanks to God?

What are some of the attributes or characteristics of God that you are thankful for?

Proclamation for a National Thanksgiving by George Washington, 1789

Whereas it is the duty of all nations to acknowledge the providence of Almighty God, to obey His will, to be grateful for His benefits, and humbly to implore His protection and favor; and whereas both Houses of Congress have, by their joint committee, requested me "to recommend to the people of the United States a day of public thanksgiving and prayer, to be observed by acknowledging with grateful hearts the many and signal favors of Almighty God, especially by affording them an opportunity peaceably to establish a form of government for their safety and happiness."

Now, therefore, I do recommend and assign Thursday, the twenty-sixth day of November next, to be devoted by the people of these states to the service of that great and glorious Being who is the beneficent Author of all the good that was, that is, or that will be; that we may then all unite in rendering unto Him our sincere and humble thanks for His kind care and protection of the people of this country previous to their becoming a nation; for the signal and manifold mercies, and the favorable interpositions of His providence, in the course and conclusion of the late war; for the great degree of tranquility, union, and plenty, which we have since enjoyed; for the peaceable and rational manner in which we have been enabled to establish constitutions of government for our safety and happiness, and particularly the national one now lately instituted; for the civil and religious liberty with which we are blessed, and the means we have of acquiring and diffusing useful knowledge; and, in general, for all the great and various favors which he has been pleased to confer upon us.

And also that we may then unite in most humbly offering our prayers and supplications to the great Lord and Ruler of Nations, and beseech Him to pardon our national and other transgressions; to enable us all, whether in public or private stations, to perform our several and relative duties properly and punctually; to render our national government a blessing to all the people, by constantly being a government of wise, just, and constitutional laws, discreetly and faithfully executed and obeyed; to protect and guide all sovereigns and nations (especially such as have shewn kindness to us), and to bless them with good governments, peace, and concord; to promote the knowledge and practice of true religion and virtue, and the increase of science among them and us; and generally to grant unto all mankind such a degree of temporal prosperity as He alone knows to be best.

Given under my hand, at the City of New York, the third day of October, in the year of our Lord one thousand seven hundred and eighty-nine.

National Thanksgiving Proclamation by Abraham Lincoln, 1863

The year that is drawing towards its close has been filled with the blessings of fruitful fields and healthful skies. To these bounties, which are so constantly enjoyed that we are prone to forget the source from which they come, others have been added, which are of so extraordinary a nature, that they cannot fail to penetrate and soften even the heart which is habitually insensible to the ever watchful providence of Almighty God.

In the midst of a civil war of unequalled magnitude and severity, which has sometimes seemed to invite and provoke the aggression of foreign states, peace has been preserved with all nations, order has been maintained, the laws have been respected and obeyed, and harmony has prevailed everywhere, except in the theater of military conflict; while that theater has been greatly contracted by the advancing armies and navies of the Union.

The needful diversions of wealth and strength from the fields of peaceful industry to the national defense have not arrested the plough, the shuttle, or the ship. The axe has enlarged the borders of our settlements, and the mines, as well of iron and coal as of the precious metals, have yielded even more abundantly than heretofore. Population has steadily increased, notwithstanding the waste that has been made in the camp, the siege and the battlefield; and the country, rejoicing in the consequences of augmented strength and vigor, is permitted to expect continuance of years with large increase of freedom.

No human counsel hath devised, nor hath any mortal hand worked out these great things. They are the gracious gifts of the Most High God, who, while dealing with us in anger for our sins, hath nevertheless remembered mercy.

It has seemed to me fit and proper that they should be solemnly, reverently and gratefully acknowledged as with one heart and voice by the whole American people; I do, therefore, invite my fellow-citizens in every part of the United States, and also those who are at sea and those who are sojourning in foreign lands, to set apart and observe the last Thursday of November next as a Day of Thanksgiving and Prayer to our beneficent Father, who dwelleth in the heavens. And I recommend to them that, while offering up the ascriptions justly due to Him for such singular deliverances and blessings; they do also, with humble penitence for our national perverseness and disobedience, commend to His tender care all those who have become widows, orphans, mourners or sufferers in the lamentable civil strife in which we are unavoidably engaged, and fervently implore the interposition of the Almighty hand to heal the wounds of the nation and to restore it, as soon as may be consistent with the Divine purposes, to the full enjoyment of peace, harmony, tranquility, and union.

In testimony whereof I have hereunto set my hand and caused the seal of the United States to be affixed.

Done at the city of Washington this third day of October, in the year of our Lord one thousand eight hundred and sixty-three, and of the Independence of the United States the eighty-eighth."

Thanksgiving Proclamation

3 Days Until Thanksgiving

Thankfullest Thanksgiving
By Pauline Shackleford Colyar, 1896

"Day after tomorrow will be Thanksgiving," said Walter, taking his seat beside Grandpa Davis on the top step of the front porch.

"And no turkey for dinner, neither," retorted Grandma Davis, while her bright steel needles clicked in and out of the sock she was knitting.

The old man was whittling a toy soldier for Walter and sat for a moment with his eyes fixed meditatively upon the blue hills massed in the distance.

"Have we got so poor as all that, Mother?" he asked, after a while, glancing over his shoulder at his wife, who was rocking to and fro just behind him.

"I'm obleeged to own to the truth," answered the old lady dejectedly. "What with the wild varmints in the woods and one thing an' another, I'm about cleaned out of all the poultry I ever had. It's downright disheartenin'."

"Well, then," asserted Grandpa Davis, with an unmirthful chuckle, "it don't appear to me as we've got so powerful much to be thankful about this year."

"Why, Grandpa!" cried Walter, in shocked surprise, "I never did hear you talk like that before."

"Never had so much call to do it, mebbe," interposed the old man cynically.

The last rays of the setting sun touched the two silvered heads and rested there like a benediction, before disappearing below the horizon.

Silence had fallen upon the little group, and a bullfrog down in the fishpond was croaking dismally.

"Why don't you go hunting, and try to kill you a turkey for Thanksgiving?" ventured Walter, slipping his arm through his grandfather's. "I saw a great big flock of wild ones down on the branch last week, and I got right close up to them before they flew."

"I reckon there ought to be a smart sight of game round and about them cane brakes along that branch," said the old man slowly, as though thinking aloud. "It used to be ahead of any strip of woods in all these parts, when me and Rick was boys. But nobody ain't hunted there, to my knowledge, not since me and him fell out."

"I wish you and Grandpa Dun were friends," sighed Walter. "It does seem too bad to have two grandpas living right side by side, and not speaking."

"I ain't got no ill-will in my heart for Rick," replied Grandpa Davis, "but he is too everlastin' hard-headed to knock under, and I'll be blamed if I go more'n halfway toward makin' up."

"That's just exactly what Grandpa Dun says about you," Walter assured him very earnestly.

"Wouldn't wonder if he did," said the old man pointedly. "Rick is always been a mighty hand to talk, and he'd drap dead in his tracks if he couldn't get in the last word."

Be this as it might, the breach had begun when the Davis cattle broke down the worn fence and demolished the Dun crop of corn, and it widened when the Dun hogs found their way through an old water gap and rooted up a field of the Davis sweet potatoes. Several times similar depredations were repeated, and then shotguns were used on both sides with telling effect. The climax was reached when John Dun eloped with Rebecca, the only child of the Davis's.

The young couple were forbidden their respective homes, though the farm they rented was scarce half a mile away, and the weeks rolled into months without a sign of their parents relenting.

When Walter was born, however, the two grandmothers stole over, without their husbands' knowledge, and mingled their tears in happy communion over the tiny blue-eyed mite.

It was a memorable day at each of the houses when the sturdy little fellow made his way, unbidden and unattended, to pay his first call, and ever afterward (though they would not admit it, even to themselves) the grandfathers watched for his coming, and vied with each other in trying to win the highest place in his young affections.

He had inherited characteristics of each of his grandsires, and possessed the bold, masterful manner which was common to them both.

"Say, Grandpa," he urged, "go hunting tomorrow and try to kill a turkey for Thanksgiving, won't you? I know Grandma would feel better to have one, and if you make a cane caller, like Papa does, I'll bet you can get a shot at one sure."

The old man did not commit himself about going, but when Walter saw him take down his gun from the pegs on the wall across which it had lain for so many years, and began to rub the barrels and oil the hammers, he went home satisfied that he had scored another victory.

Perhaps nothing less than his grandson's pleading could have induced Grandpa Davis to visit again the old hunting ground which had been so dear to him in bygone days, which was so rich in hallowed memories. It seemed almost a desecration of the happy past to hunt there now alone.

The first cold streaks of dawn were just stealing into the sky the next morning when, armed with shot-pouch, powder-flask, and his old double-barreled gun, Grandpa Davis made his way toward the branch. A medley of bird notes filled the air, long streamers of gray moss floated out from the swaying trees, and showers of autumn leaves fluttered down to earth. Some of the cows were grazing outside the pen, up to their hocks in lush, fresh grass, while others lay on the ground contentedly chewing their cuds. All of them raised their heads and looked at him as he passed by.

How like old times it was to be up at daybreak for a hunt! The long years seemed suddenly to have rolled away, leaving him once more a boy. He almost wondered why Rick had not whistled to him as he used to do. Rick was an early riser, and somehow always got ready before he did.

There was an alertness in the old man's face and a spring in his step as he lived over in thought the joyous days of his childhood. The clouds were flushed with pink when he came in sight of the big water oak on the margin of the stream, and recollected how he and Rick had loved to go swimming in the deep, clear water beneath its shade.

"We used to run every step of the way," he soliloquized, laughing, "unbuttonin' as we went, chuck our clothes on the bank, and 'most break our necks tryin' to git in the water fust. I've got half a notion to take a dip this mornin', if it wasn't quite so cool," he went on, but a timely twinge of rheumatism brought him to his senses, and he seated himself on the roots of a convenient tree.

Cocking his gun, he laid it across his knees and waited there motionless, imitating the yelp of a turkey the while. Three or four small canes, graduated in size, and fitted firmly one into the other, enabled him to make the note, and so expert had he become by long practice that the deception was perfect.

After a pause he repeated the call; then came another pause, another call, and over in the distance there sounded an answer. How the blood coursed through the old man's veins as he listened! There it was again. It was coming nearer, but very slowly. He wondered how many were in the flock, and called once more. This time, to his surprise, an answer came from a different direction—a long, rasping sound, a sort of cross between a cock's crow and a turkey's yelp.

He started involuntarily and very cautiously peeped around. Hardly twenty steps from him another gray head protruded itself from the hole of another tree, and Grandpa Davis and Grandpa Dun looked into each other's eyes.

"I'll be double-jumped-up if that ain't Rick!" cried Grandpa Davis, under his breath. "And there ain't a turkey as ever wore a feather that he could fool. A minute more, and he'll spoil the fun. Rick," he commanded, "stop that racket and sneak over here by me," beckoning mysteriously. "Sh-h-h! They are answerin' ag'in. Down on your marrow-bones whilst I call."

Flattening himself upon the ground as nearly as he could, and creeping behind the undergrowth, Grandpa Dun made his way laboriously to the desired spot. He had never excelled in calling turkeys, but he was a far better shot than Grandpa Davis.

Without demur the two old boys fell naturally into the role of former days. Breathless and excited, they crouched there, waiting for the fateful moment. Their nerves were tense, their eyes dilated, and their hearts beating like hammers.

Grandpa Davis had continued to call, and now the answer was very near.

"Gimme the first shot, Billy," whispered Grandpa Dun. "I let you do the callin'; and, besides, you know you never could hit nothin' that wasn't as big as the side of a meetin' house."

Before Grandpa Davis had time to reply, there came the "put-put-put" which signals possible danger. A stately gobbler raised his head to reconnoiter; two guns were fired almost simultaneously, and, with a whir and a flutter, the flock disappeared in the cane brake.

The two old boys bounded over the intervening sticks and stumps with an agility that Walter himself might have envied, and bending over the prostrate gobbler exclaimed in concert, "Ain't he a dandy, though!"

They examined him critically, cutting out his beard as a trophy, and measured the spread of his wings.

"But he's yourn, after all, Rick," said Grandpa Davis ruefully. "These here ain't none of my shot, so I reckon I must have missed him."

"I knowed you would, Billy, afore your fired," Grandpa Dun replied, with mock gravity. "He's big enough for us to go halvers and both have plenty. More'n that, you done the callin' anyhow."

Then they laughed, and as they looked into one another's faces, each seemed to realize for the first time that his former chum was an old man.

A moment before they had been two rollicking boys off on a lark together and in the twinkling of an eye they had changed into Walter's two grandfathers, who had not spoken to each other since years before the lad was born.

A Good Thanksgiving
by Marian Douglas, 1915

Said old Gentleman Gray, "On a Thanksgiving Day,
If you want a good time, then give something away,"
So he sent a fat turkey to Shoemaker Price,
And the shoemaker said, "What a big bird! How nice!
And, since a good dinner's before me, I ought
To give poor Widow Lee the small chicken I bought."
"This fine chicken, oh, see!" said the pleased Widow Lee,
"And the kindness that sent it, how precious to me!
I would like to make some one as happy as I
I'll give Washwoman Biddy my big pumpkin pie."
"And oh, sure," Biddy said, "'tis the queen of all pies!
Just to look at its yellow face gladdens my eyes!
Now it's my turn, I think; and a sweet ginger-cake
For the motherless Finigan children I'll bake."
"A sweet cake, all our own! 'Tis too good to be true!"
Said the Finigan children, Rose, Denny, and Hugh;
"It smells sweet of spice, and we'll carry a slice
To poor little Lame Jake—who has nothing that's nice."
"Oh, I thank you, and thank you!" said little Lame Jake;
"Oh, what bootiful, bootiful, bootiful cake!
And oh, such a big slice! I will save all the crumbs,
And will give 'em to each little sparrow that comes!"
And the sparrows they twittered, as if they would say,
Like old Gentleman Gray, "On a Thanksgiving Day,
If you want a good time, then give something away!"

Yet the humor of the situation was irresistible after all, and, without knowing just how it happened, or which made the first advance, Rick and Billy found themselves still laughing until the tears coursed down their furrowed cheeks, and shaking hands with as much vigor as though each one had been working a pump handle.

"I'll tell you what it is, Billy," said Rick at last, "you all come over to my house, and we'll eat him together on Thanksgiving."

"See here, Rick," suggested Billy, abstracting a nickel from his trousers' pocket; "heads at your house, and tails at mine."

"All right," came the hearty response.

Billy tossed the coin into the air. It struck a twig and hid itself among the fallen leaves, where they sought it in vain.

"'Tain't settled yet," announced Rick, "but lemme tell you what let's do. S'posin' we all go over tomorrow—it'll be Thanksgivin', you know—and eat him at John's house."

"Good!" cried Billy, with beaming face. "You always did have a head for thinkin' up things, Rick, and this here'll sorter split the difference, and ease matters so as—"

"Yes, and our wives can draw straws, if they've got a mind to, and see which of them is obligated to make the fust call," interrupted Rick.

"Jist heft him, old feller," urged one of them.

"Ain't he a whopper, though!" exclaimed the other.

"Have a peppermint, Rick?" asked Billy, offering some of his favorite candy.

"Don't keer if I do," agreed Rick, who popped it into his mouth.

Seating themselves upon a fallen hickory log, they expectorated, recalling old times, and enjoying their laugh with the careless freedom of their childhood days.

"Rick, do your ricolleck the fight you and a coon had out on the limb of that tree over yonder, one night?" queried Billy, nudging his companion in the ribs. "He come mighty nigh gittin' the best of you."

"He tore one sleeve out of my jacket, and Mammy gimme a beatin' besides," chuckled Rick. "And say, Billy, wasn't it fun the day we killed old man Lee's puddle ducks for wild ones? I don't believe I ever run as fast in my life."

Thus, one adventure recalled another, and the two old boys laughed uproariously, clapping their hands and holding their sides, while the sun climbed up among the treetops.

"Ain't we been two old fools to stay mad all this time?" asked one of them, and the other readily agreed that they had, as they once more grasped hands before parting.

Walter had arranged the Thanksgiving surprise for his parents, but when he brought home the big gobbler, he was unable longer to keep the secret and divulged his share in what had happened.

"I didn't really believe either one of them could hit a turkey," he confided to his father, "but I wanted to have them meet once more, for I knew if they did they would make friends."

The parlor was odorous with late fall roses next morning, the table set, and Walter and his parents in gala attire, when two couples, walking arm in arm, appeared upon the stretch of white road leading up to the front gate.

One couple was slightly in advance of the other, and Grandpa Davis, who was behind, whispered to his wife, "Listen, Mary, Rick is actually tryin' to sing, and he never could turn a tune, but somehow it does warm up my heart to hear him: seems like old times ag'in."

After dinner was over—and such a grand dinner it was—Grandpa Davis voiced the sentiment of the rest of the happy family party when he announced, quite without warning, "Well, this here has been the thankfullest Thanksgiving I ever seen, and I hope the good Lord will spar' us all for yet a few more."

Recipes

Below are two of my favorite Thanksgiving recipes. Thanksgiving wouldn't be the same at the Puetz house without them. ~Amy

Grandma's Angel Biscuits

2 cups milk
2 Tbsp. lemon juice or vinegar
2½ cups whole-wheat flour
2½ cups white flour
3 tsp. baking powder
1 tsp. baking soda
1 tsp. salt
3 Tbsp. sugar
1 Tbsp. (or 1 package) yeast dissolved in ½ cup warm water
¾ cup butter

Mix the milk and lemon juice (or vinegar) and set aside for about 5 minutes. This will sour the milk. In a large bowl combine all the dry ingredients and cut in the butter with a pastry blender until it resembles crumbs. Stir the yeast in the warm water until dissolved. Make a well in the center of the dry ingredients, and pour the soured milk and yeast in at the same time, and stir to combine until the flour mixture is moistened. Place a cover over the bowl and refrigerate for about an hour. Remove the dough from the bowl onto a floured surface. Sprinkle a little flour on top of the dough and roll out to a thickness of about ½ inch and cut biscuits with a biscuit cutter. Place on an ungreased cookie sheet about an inch apart. Bake in a 400° F oven for about 12 minutes.

Oatmeal Pie

uncooked pie crust
2 eggs, beaten
¾ cup corn syrup
¾ cup sugar
¾ cup quick oats
½ cup margarine or butter softened
1 tsp. vanilla

Stir all ingredients until well combined. Pour into an unbaked pie crust. Bake at 350° F for about 40 to 45 minutes. When a knife inserted near the center comes out clean, the pie is done.

2 Days Until Thanksgiving

Turning the Thanksgiving Tables
By Carolyn Sherwin Bailey, 1918

None of the scholars in the Blake School liked to have the orphans attend it.

The arrangement by which the long line of "all-alone" boys and girls in their "all-alike" blue suits and long blue dresses took their way every morning from the Orphans' Home and came to the brick school building had only been made that fall. Chester was a comfortable little town, its tree-lined streets stretching lazily along until they ended in fertile fields and farm lands outside the village limits. Almost everyone owned a home, and the children did not know what it meant to be poor and an orphan. They somehow resented the fact that the big white Orphans' Home was a part of Chester.

"They ought to live out in the country somewhere," Dorothy Turner, the history teacher's little daughter, said, as she moved away from the school gate to let the orphans in one morning in November. "I'm sure they would be happier, for they must feel that they don't belong here with us."

"I know it. They do look so different," Alice Harding, whose father was Chester's mayor, added. "It must be mortifying to dress just like everybody else," she continued.

The orphans did make a marked contrast to the others as they filed in the gate and through the school door. Dorothy's red felt hat could not keep her fair curls from blowing about her fairer face, and her matching red coat was so long as to reach past the bottom of her skirt. Alice wore a pink hat with elaborate ribbons above her stylish curly hair, and her hunter green coat was fringed with delicate lace.

The two girls must have looked very winsome and attractive to the orphans. One little girl in blue at the end of the line stepped away from the others and went timidly up to Dorothy and Alice. She put out one hand and touched the lovely lace on Alice's coat shyly, as if even the touch of it were a delight. Alice drew away a little, but a faint flush of shame tinged her cheek, as the girl shrank back, almost as if she had been struck, and took her place in line.

"That's Molly Baxter," Dorothy said. "She's going to be at the head of our class before the year is out. Father says the Baxter family, away back, came over in the *Mayflower*, but there's nobody left now except Molly, and there's no money either, so she had to go on the town. I don't suppose she ever had anything to wear so pretty as your coat in all her life."

"It's too bad, isn't it?" Alice said with a kinder note in her voice. "She looks like a little Pilgrim girl, doesn't she, in that long blue dress and white hood?"

"Oh, that makes me think of next week—Thanksgiving Day, Alice, and we're going to have such a dinner!" Dorothy exclaimed, laughing happily, as the two friends locked arms and went into the schoolroom.

The whole atmosphere of the school was charged with the spirit of the coming holiday. The scholars had brought great branches of oak and maple covered with bright leaves to twine the school pictures of "The First Thanksgiving" and the "Pilgrims Going to Church." Sprays of orange bittersweet filled a brass jar on the teacher's desk, and a bunch of grain had been put outside of one of the windows to attract the birds.

It was history day. Dorothy's father, Professor Turner, stood on the platform and, after the opening exercises, took charge of the class.

"I want some one to recite the story of the Pilgrims' first Thanksgiving better than it has ever been recited before in the Blake School," he said. "Who will try?"

No one volunteered for a moment, not even Dorothy. Then a timid hand went up in the back of the room.

"Good!" Professor Turner said. "Molly Baxter ought to recite very well, for she comes of a Pilgrim family."

It seemed to little orphan Molly that twice the number of eyes pierced her that really did, as she stood up. She had loved the history lesson that told of the great, first family gathering for thanksgiving so long ago in New England. It had thrilled lonely Molly to the very heart, for it seemed so full of the plenty and love that had been denied her. As she began to recite, Molly's voice faltered. Then she forgot everything but her interest in the story. The class sat as still as mice, as they listened to the rise and fall of the little orphan girl's sweet voice.

"The days of spring and summer flew by," she said, "and autumn came to the Pilgrims. Never, in Holland or England, had they seen the like of the treasures that nature had given them. Their little farm plots had been blessed by sunshine and shower, so the Pilgrims, rejoicing, reaped their fruits, and housed them for the winter. They were filled with the spirit of thanksgiving, and so they decided to hold the first harvest-home in New England.

"For a week they rested from work and feasted, and for three days they entertained the Indians. And the Indians brought them corn and venison, so all made merry together.

"It was a royal feast that the Pilgrims spread that first golden autumn, a feast worthy of their Indian guests. Kettles, skillets, and spits were overworked, and the knives and spoons made merry music on the pewter plates. The good governor put the vegetables that graced the table into rhyme. He said:

> "'All sorts of grain which our own land doth yield,
> Was hither brought, and sown in every field;
> As wheat and rye, barley, oats, beans, and peas,
> Here all thrive, and we profit from them raise.
> All sorts of roots and herbs in gardens grow,
> Parsnips, carrots, turnips, or what you'll sow,
> Onions, melons, cucumbers, radishes,
> Potatoes, beets, rhubarb and fair cabbages.'

"All the Pilgrims' jealousies and discontent were forgotten that first Thanksgiving Day. It made them better and braver to rest awhile and give thanks together. And it was a promise of other Thanksgivings to come."

Professor Turner did not try to hush the subdued exclamations of pleasure from the class that followed Molly's last words. Neither did he try to stop the round of applause that came as she sat down. No one but Molly could have told the Thanksgiving story with so much feeling and charm. Even the orphans realized that as they sat up straighter with their pride that Molly belonged to them. All during the rest of the session the class found it difficult to settle down to problems in greatest common division and dry measure. In imagination they were Pilgrim children of long ago, measuring the good fruits and grains of the first harvest and spreading the Thanksgiving table to share them with the Indians, that first harvest-home.

Alice was waiting for Dorothy outside the school door at the end of the session.

"I've had a perfectly splendid idea for Thanksgiving, Dorothy," she said. Then she whispered something in her friend's ear. Dorothy listened intently, and then her face dimpled into a smile of delight.

"Oh, I think that would be lovely!" she said. "We'll do it. Tell the girls to meet at my house tomorrow afternoon to talk it over and ask them to wear their Camp Fire dresses. That will make it seem all the more real."

The two girls went out of the gate and up the road together. They had to pass the line of orphans, going home two by two, and Dorothy called, "Molly, oh, goodbye, Molly!"

The little girl in blue turned, hardly believing that the pleasant words were meant for her. When she saw that they really were, for both Dorothy and Alice were waving their hands to her, a smile of joy lighted her face.

"Goodbye. Thank you"—she half breathed the last.

"Why, she's really pretty, isn't she?" Dorothy said. "I never noticed how blue her eyes are."

"And her hair wants to curl," Alice said, "only they make her braid it all the time."

Thanksgiving was a real picture day. Enough bright leaves were left to give it color, and the sky was blue, without a cloud. The golden sunshine made even the stubble in the fields gleam, and the air was pungent with the odors of fruit, and vegetables, and bonfires.

It was like every other day at the Orphans' Home though. There was the same routine of getting up and dressing and going down to breakfast by rule and time from the big dormitories. The orphans would not go to school, but certain tasks were detailed to them that would fill the morning. There would be spareribs and applesauce for dinner, with an orange for each child for dessert, but the table would still be bare of linen and set with the same thick white crockery and tin mugs. And it would not be a family feast for these little "all-alone" children.

Molly was all alive with the spirit of the day, though. Her eyes shone, and she burst into bits of song as she washed the faces and hands of the little ones and combed their hair before breakfast.

"It's my day!" she kept saying over and over to herself. "I'm one of the Thanksgiving children."

The thought sweetened Molly's breakfast porridge and made her fingers fly as she pared apples in the kitchen afterward.

"I'm pretending that it's the first harvest-home," she said to herself, "and I'm getting ready for the dinner. There is ever so much to do because all those Indians are coming to share it with us. Why—" Molly looked out of the window at the sunny road, and then rubbed her eyes to see if she were dreaming. No, it was quite true; she could believe her eyes. Down the road toward the Orphan's Home marched a long line of Indians, brave in moccasins, fringed dresses, blankets and beaded headbands. They were everyday Indians, though, and carried, each one, a bag or basket. Dorothy and Alice led the line. They were the girls of the Blake School dressed in their Camp Fire costumes, and come to turn the Thanksgiving tables at the Orphans' Home. It was the Indians who would spread the feast for these small Pilgrims who were as much alone and in need of friendship as those who came over in the *Mayflower*.

Molly ran out to meet them, and Dorothy came up to her with outstretched arms.

"It's all arranged with the matron," she explained. "We girls have brought over a Thanksgiving dinner, and we're going to set the table, and stay and eat it with you, and then play games in the afternoon. You are to help us, Molly, and it's going to be such fun!"

It was the best fun that the orphans had ever had. In almost no time the tables in the dining room were covered with snow-white cloths, along the edge of which the Camp Fire girls fastened trailing vines covered with crimson and yellow leaves. The wooden bowls from the kitchen were filled with rosy apples, purple grapes, russet pears, and nuts. The roasted turkeys and chickens that the girls had brought needed only to be warmed in the oven to send out their delicious aroma. There were little individual pumpkin pies and mince pies and frosted cakes for all the orphans, and even a package of homemade fudge for each, tied with an orange ribbon and a spray of bittersweet.

The Camp Fire girls, with Molly's help, served the food and then slipped into their places between the orphans. It was surprising how easy it was to get acquainted with each other over the feast, and the tables looked just like the pictures of the first Thanksgiving dinner, the Indians in their bright costumes sharing it with their more plainly dressed neighbors.

The rule of no talking at meals that was established at the home was lifted for this happy day, and the dining room became suddenly alive with merry voices. When the feast was over, Dorothy led them all into the big living room, where an open fire was burning, and played the piano for singing, Molly leading them, for she could sing as well as recite history. The walls rang with "America," "Over the River and Through the Woods," "Columbia," and the old German hymn, "We Plough the Fields and Scatter the Good Seed in the Land." Then they played Blind Man's Bluff, Going to Jerusalem, Cat in the Corner, and the Farmer in the Dell, until the short afternoon began to settle into golden dusk, and the setting sun told the Camp Fire girls that it was time for them to go home.

"We've had a beautiful time," Alice said. "So have we!" shouted a chorus of orphans.

"And we think we will come over every Saturday afternoon and see you," Dorothy said.

It was such good news that the Camp Fire girls could hardly say goodbye because of the applause.

"Wasn't it a nice Thanksgiving?" Alice asked as the girls went home, like a real band of Indians, between the field and trees.

"The best ever," Dorothy said, emphatically. "And aren't the orphan nice?" she finished, happily.

Thanksgiving Games

This story mentions several of the good old-fashioned games of long ago. These games are still lots of fun to play today! Below are the instructions on how to play Going to Jerusalem (which is similar to musical chairs) and The Farmer in the Dell.

Going to Jerusalem
By Ethel Perrin, 1902

Stools, one less than the number of players are placed in a circle. The player who is "it" stands on the stool in the middle of the circle while the other players march round outside the ring. At a given signal all the players try to seat themselves on the stools in the circle. The one who is left without a seat is "it," and stands on the center stool, while the players march again. Chairs or small rugs may be used instead of stools.

The Farmer in the Dell
By Harry Sperling, 1916

This may be played with any number of people. The children form a circle, facing center, hands joined. One of the children, the farmer, stands in the center of the ring. The ring moves continuously to the left as the children say, "The farmer in the dell. The farmer in the dell. Heigh-o, the derry-o! The farmer in the dell."

Next the group says, "The farmer takes a wife. The farmer takes a wife, Heigh-o, the derry-o! The farmer takes a wife." The player in the center chooses one from the circle, who leaves her place and stands with the first player. At each new stanza the child last chosen beckons to another. Thus, the wife takes a child, the child takes a nurse, the nurse takes a cat, the cat takes a rat, and the rat, who chooses last, takes a child to be the cheese.

When all have been brought into the circle, the children begin saying all the verses over again. The lines of each verse now are, "The farmer runs away. The farmer runs away. Heigh-o, the derry-o! The farmer runs away." Followed by, "The wife runs away. The child runs away. The nurse runs away. The cat runs away. The rat runs away."

The cheese now stands alone, whereupon the children stop marching and call to the child who is the cheese, "The cheese stands alone. The cheese stands alone. Heigh-o, the derry-o! The cheese stands alone."

The game now begins again with the cheese becoming the new farmer in the center.

1 Day Until Thanksgiving

Squanto
By Mr. Blaisdell and Mr. Ball, 1913

One Friday afternoon in March, a tall Indian came out of the woods at the top of the hill. He walked boldly toward Plymouth and cried out, "Welcome, Englishmen, welcome!"

It seems that the Indian's name was Samoset and that he had lived on the coast of Maine, where he picked up a few English words from the fishermen.

The Pilgrims treated their unexpected guest kindly. They gave him a coat to cover his bare shoulders, and they fed him biscuits, butter, cheese, pudding, and roast duck.

Samoset was so pleased with his new friends that he came back the following week. He brought another Indian with him. The name of this Indian was Squanto, a sort of nickname for Squantum or Tisquantum.

It seems that Squanto had once lived in this region, but had been kidnapped by a cruel English captain named Hunt. This captain planned to sell Squanto as a slave in Spain. But just as Squanto was to be auctioned off, a kind monk arrived and saved him. The monk helped Squanto travel to England. He lived in London and learned to speak English pretty well. Then a kindhearted sea captain brought him back and put him ashore on the coast of Maine.

He traveled back to his native home only to find most of his people dead. Squanto said that many Indians once lived in this region and had large fields of corn, but some dreadful disease had broken out, from which nearly all of them died. The place the white men had built their town was the exact location that Squanto's village used to stand.

Squanto was a useful friend to the Pilgrims from the very beginning. He took them out to a little river close by and showed them how to fish for eels. He stomped the eels out of the mud and caught them with his hands. Governor Bradford says in his journal, "The eels were fat and sweet, and our people were glad of them."

Shortly afterwards, Squanto came to live with the Pilgrims. It would be a long story to tell you all this Indian did for his half-starved friends.

When the Pilgrims made their first trip along the shore of Cape Cod, they found several basketfuls of corn, which the Indians had buried in the sand. When they found the Indians who had left the corn, they paid them for it. They saved enough of this to plant in the spring. Squanto now taught them how to get the old Indian cornfield ready for a new crop.

The people at Plymouth did not know how to plant the corn they had found, but Squanto taught them. By watching the trees, Squanto knew when to put their corn into the ground. When the young leaf of the white oak tree was as large as a squirrel's ear, he knew that it was time to put the corn into the ground. Squanto taught the white people how to catch fish that were used to make their corn grow. They put one or two fish into each hill of corn, but they had to watch the cornfield day and night for two weeks after planting. If they had not watched it, the wolves would dig up the fish and the corn with them.

The white people learned also to cook their corn as the Indians did. They learned to eat hominy and succotash, and these we still call by their Indian names. Of all the plants that grew in America, Indian corn was the most important to the Indians. It was also of the most value to the first white people who came to this country.

It has been said that without the seed corn and the help of Squanto, the whole Plymouth settlement would have starved to death before the end of the first year. The Pilgrims had left their old home in England without hooks and lines for fishing. Here again Squanto was able to lend a hand and taught his friends how to catch fish and lobsters the Indian way.

Squanto then began to serve the settlers in another way. The chief of the Indians in the Plymouth region was Massasoit. He had been told wonderful things about the white-faced strangers and wished to visit them. One day he came with some of his warriors to the top of the hill to make a friendly visit, and Squanto was sent out to talk with him. Shortly afterward Massasoit and twenty warriors came walking into the settlement, leaving their bows and arrows behind them. This Indian chief was a tall, strong man. He wore a large chain of white bone beads about his neck. At the back of his neck hung a little bag of tobacco, which he smoked and gave to the Pilgrims to smoke. His face was painted a deep red; his head and face were so covered with oil that he looked greasy. His warriors were tall and strong and were painted, some black, some red, some yellow, and some white.

The chief and his warriors went marching slowly along the narrow street and into the meeting house. A great noise was made with a trumpet, and some of the men fired their muskets. Governor Bradford did the honors. He kissed the chief's hand, and Massasoit kissed the governor, and then they sat down for a talk. The Indian chief sat on a green mat with some cushions placed round him.

Massasoit was greatly pleased with his welcome. A copper chain and some beads were given to him. He said he would live in peace with his white-faced friends. The Indian chief kept his word. The treaty was kept sacred for about fifty years.

The Pilgrims looked upon Squanto as, "a special instrument sent of God for their good beyond their expectation," as Bradford said.

The Pilgrims owed a good deal of money to some men in England, for they had borrowed money to buy food and supplies for the journey. After a while, they coasted along the shore to trade with the Indians for furs and corn. On such trips Squanto was a great help as pilot. Late one fall about two years after Squanto came to live with the Pilgrims, he sailed with his friends outside of Cape Cod as far as the elbow. This place is now known as Chatham. Here the Indians were shy of the strangers, but Squanto at last got them to sell eight hogsheads of corn and beans.

Poor Squanto! On this trip he came down with a fever and died in a few days. Before he died he gave some of his things to his English friends as keepsakes. His last words were, "Pray that the Indian Squanto may go to the white man's heaven."

The Landing of the Pilgrims
By Mrs. Hemans, 1888

The breaking waves dashed high
On a stern and rockbound coast,
And the woods, against a stormy sky,
Their giant branches tossed;

And the heavy night hung dark
The hills and waters o'er,
When a band of exiles moored their bark
On the wild New England shore.

Not as the conqueror comes,
They, the true-hearted, came;
Not with the roll of stirring drums,
And the trumpet that sings of fame;

Not as the flying come,
In silence and in fear;
They shook the depths of the desert's gloom
With their hymns of lofty cheer.

Amidst the storm they sang,
Till the stars heard, and the sea;
And the sounding aisles of the dim woods rang
To the anthem of the free.

The ocean-eagle soared
From his nest by the white wave's foam,
And the rocking pines of the forest roared;
This was their welcome home.

There were men with silver hair
Amidst that Pilgrim band;
Why had they come to wither there,
Away from their childhood's land?

There was woman's fearless eye,
Lit by her deep love's truth;
There was manhood's brow serenely high,
And the fiery heart of youth.

What sought they thus afar?
Bright jewels of the mine?
The wealth of seas? The spoils of war?
They sought a faith's pure shrine.

Ay, call it holy ground,
The land where first they trod!
They have left unstained what there they found,
Freedom to worship God!

Thanksgiving Song

We Thank Thee

Sing the songs below and discuss what they mean.

Anonymous   Arranged from Herman Kotzschmar

1. We thank thee, O our Father, For all thy loving care;
We thank thee that thou madest The world so bright and fair.
We thank thee for the sunshine, And for the pleasant showers; And,
O our God, we thank thee, We thank thee for the flowers.

2. Out in the sunny meadows, And in the woodlands cool,
Upon the breezy hillside, And by each reedy pool,
And in the quiet pasture, And by the broad highway; All
pure, and fresh, and stainless, They spring up every day.

3. And in the dusty city, Where busy crowds pass by,
And where the tall dark houses Stand up and hide the sky,
And where through lanes and alleys No pleasant breezes blow, E'en
there, O God our Father, Thou mak'st the flowers grow.

4. And whether in the city, Or in the fields they dwell;
Always the same sweet message The fair sweet flowers tell.
For they are all so wonderful, They show thy power abroad; And
they are all so beautiful, They tell thy love, O God. A-MEN.

Countdown to Thanksgiving   Amy Puetz

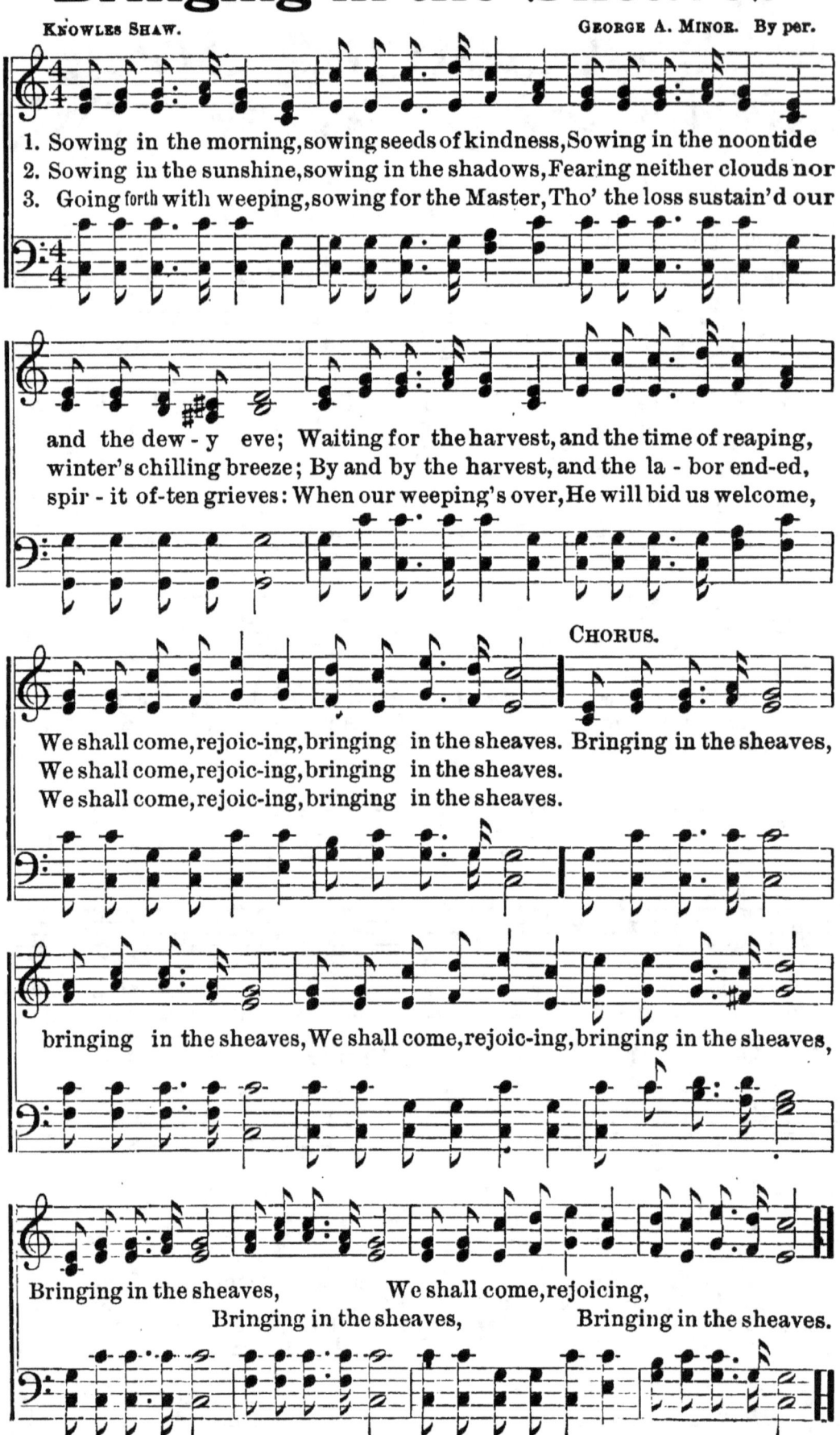

Thanksgiving

A Turkey for the Stuffing

By Katherine Grace Hulbert, 1921

It always made Ben feel solemn to watch the river in a storm. Today it was gray and rough and noisy, and the few boats which went down toward Lake Huron pitched about so that their decks slanted first one way, then another, and their sides were coated with ice.

"Gran'ma, what day's today?" he asked at last, turning from the stormy river to glance about their warm, comfortable, little room.

"Wednesday, Benny," answered the small old woman who crouched over the stove.

"Then tomorrow will be Thanksgiving Day, and the Ross family are going to have a turkey," said Ben excitedly. "What are we going to have, Gran'ma?"

Mrs. Moxon looked over her glasses at her grandson's small, thin figure in its patched and faded clothes, and at his bright, eager face. "Sonny, dear, what do you think Gran'ma has for Thanksgiving?" she asked gently.

The expectant look faded from Ben's face, and he tried hard to keep a cheerful look on his face. He did not need to be told how bare of dainties their cupboard was, for everything there he had brought with his own hands. Bacon and smoked fish enough for all winter were stored away; flour, potatoes, and a few other vegetables were there.

"Tell me about a real Thanksgiving dinner," the small boy begged after the first disappointment had been bravely put away. Mrs. Moxon took off her spectacles and leaned back cautiously in her broken rocking chair.

"I remember one Thanksgiving when your pa was alive, we had a dinner fit for a king. There was a ten-pound turkey, with bread stuffing. I put the sage and onions into the stuffing with my own hands."

"We could have some stuffing," interrupted Ben, eagerly.

"So we could, Sonny, so we could. It takes you to think of things," and Mrs. Moxon affectionately patted the little brown hand on her knee. "It never would 'a' come to me that we might have turkey stuffing even if we didn't have any turkey."

Ben beamed with delight at this praise. "And was there anything else besides the turkey and the stuffing, Gran'ma?"

"Land, yes, child. There was turnips and mashed potatoes and mince pie, and your pa got two pounds of grapes, though grapes was expensive at that time o' year. Yes, nobody could ask for a better dinner than that was."

"We could have one just like it, all but the turkey and the mince pie and the grapes," said Ben hopefully.

"So we can, and will, too, child," answered the old woman. "Trust you for making the best of things," and the two smiled at each other happily.

Next morning Ben watched his grandmother add an egg, some sage, and chopped onion to a bowlful of dry bread, pour boiling water over it, and put the mixture in the oven.

"Your father said I made the best turkey stuffing he ever ate," she said with satisfaction. "We'll see how it comes out, Benny."

"I can hardly wait until dinner time," Ben said, with an excited skip. "I believe I'll go down to the beach, and pick up driftwood for a while. You can call me when the things are most cooked, Gran'ma."

The storm of the day before had left many a bit of board or end of a log on the beach that would be just the thing for Mrs. Moxon's stove.

Ben worked so hard that he did not notice a big barge that was coming slowly down the river, towing two other boats behind it, until he heard a voice ask, "Hullo, kid! What makes you work so hard on Thanksgiving Day?"

Then he straightened up, to see the boat's captain standing near its pilot house, and shouting through a great trumpet.

"I'm waiting for dinner to cook," Ben answered in his piping voice.

"Can't hear you!" roared the captain. "Run home and get your horn and talk to me."

Ben ran up the little hill to Mrs. Ross' house and borrowed her trumpet, or megaphone. One's voice sounds much louder when these are used, and they are to be found at every house on the shores of the St. Marys, for the people on the boats and those on the land often want to say "How do you do?" to each other. It was all Ben could do to hold the great tin trumpet straight, for it was nearly as long as he was.

"I'm waiting for dinner to cook," the boy shouted again, and this time the captain heard him.

"Going to have turkey, I suppose?" the captain asked.

"No, but we're going to have turkey stuffing," answered Ben with pride.

"Turkey stuffing but no turkey! If that isn't the best I ever heard!" The captain had dropped his trumpet and doubled up with sudden laughter.

Thankfully, Ben did not hear. "What else are you going to have?" he called when he had repeated the joke about him. "Mince pie without any mincemeat?"

"No, sir!" Ben's voice was shrill but clear. "My father had mince pie for Thanksgiving dinner once, though."

"Did he?" The captain dropped his trumpet again. "That boy's all right," he said to the first mate.

Over the River and Through the Woods
By Lydia Maria Child, 1844

Over the river and through the woods,
To Grandfather's house we go;
The horse knows the way
To carry the sleigh
Through the white and drifted snow.

Over the river and through the woods,
Oh, how the wind does blow!
It stings the toes
And bites the nose
As over the ground we go.

Over the river and through the woods,
To have a first-rate play.
Hear the bells ring
"Ting-a-ling-ling!"
Hurrah for Thanksgiving Day!

Over the river and through the woods,
Now Grandfather's cap I spy!
Hurrah for the fun!
Is the pudding done?
Hurrah for the pumpkin pie!

"He's too plucky to be laughed at. I'm going to send him some turkey for his stuffing, Morgan. Tell the cook to get ready half a turkey and a mince pie, and say, Morgan, have him send up one of those small baskets of grapes. We'll tie them to a piece of plank, and they'll float ashore all right. Tell the cook to hurry, or we'll be too far downstream for the boy to get the things." Then he raised his trumpet again. "Say, kid, can you row that boat that's tied to your dock?"

"Yes, sir."

"Well, you hurry out into the river, and I'll put off a float with some things for your Thanksgiving dinner. You're going to have some turkey for that stuffing."

You may be sure Ben lost no time in pushing the rowboat off into the stream, where the end of a plank and its delicious load were soon bobbing up and down on the water. How he did smack his lips when he lifted them into the boat, and how pleased he was for Grandma!

"First the stuffing, and then the turkey! My, ain't I blessed?" He did not know the captain had said he was plucky, and that blessings are very apt to follow pluck.

The Twilight of Thanksgiving
by William D. Kelly

The day has lengthened into eve,
And over all the meadows
The twilight's silent shuttles weave
Their somber web of shadows;
With northern lights the cloudless skies
Are faintly phosphorescent,
And just above yon wooded rise
The new moon shows her crescent

Before the evening lamps are lit,
While day and night commingle.
The sire and matron come and sit
Beside the cozy ingle;
And softly speak of the delight
Within their bosoms swelling,
Because beneath their roof tonight
Their dear ones all are dwelling.

And when around the cheerful blaze
The young folks take their places,
What blissful dreams of other days
Light up their aged faces!

The past returns with all its joys,
And they again are living,
The years in which, as girls and boys.
Their children kept Thanksgiving.

The stalwart son recalls the time
When, urged to the endeavor,
He tried the well-greased pole to climb,
And failed of fame forever.
The daughter tells of her enterprise
When, as a new beginner,
She helped her mother make the pies
For the Thanksgiving dinner.

And thus with laugh and jest and song,
And tender recollections,
Love speeds the happy hours along,
And fosters fond affections;
While Fancy, listening to the mirth,
And dreaming pleasant fictions,
Imagines through the winds on earth
That Heaven breathes benedictions.

Happy Thanksgiving

If you decided to create a play for your family, now is the day to preform it. Have fun!

Thankful Cards

Below are cards for writing down things you are thankful for. Make copies of this pages and give one to each person and let them write down their blessings.

Countdown to Thanksgiving   Amy Puetz

Index

Activities
    Thankful Cards, 87
    Thanksgiving Proclamation, 63–66
    Thanksgiving Quiz, 19
    Thanksgiving Skit, 57

Authors
    Bailey, Carolyn Sherwin, 15, 27, 73
    Baldwin, James, 55
    Blaisdell and Ball, 78
    Brown, Fannie Wilder, 45
    Coolidge, Susan, 59
    Colyar, Pauline Shackleford, 67
    Hale, Sarah Josepha, 40
    Hulbert, Katherine Grace, 83
    Leland, Emily Hewitt, 7
    Mackenzie, Robert, 32
    Miller, Olive Thorne, 48
    Puetz, Amy, 37
    Trowbridge, J. T., 20

Cooking
    Grandma's Angel Biscuits, 72
    How to Roast a Turkey, 43
    Oatmeal Pie, 72
    Pumpkin Log, 44
    Pumpkin Pie, 43

Countdown to Thanksgiving printable calendar, 6

Crafts
    Hat, 36
    Indian Headdress, 36
    Pilgrim Collar and Bonnet, 31

Excerpt from *Godey's Lady's Book Magazine*, 39

Games
    The Farmer in the Dell, 77
    Going to Jerusalem, 77
    Harvest Hunt, 6
    Thanksgiving the Game, 47

Hat, 36

Indian Headdress, 36

National Monument to the Forefathers, 35

Our National Thanksgiving Day by Sarah Hale, 40

Pilgrim Collar and Bonnet, 31

Poems
    "All Good Gifts Around Us," by Matthias Claudius, 56
    "A Good Thanksgiving" by Marian Douglas, 70
    "The Landing of the Pilgrims" by Mrs. Hemans, 80
    "Over the River and Through the Woods" by Lydia Maria Child, 85
    "Poem for Thanksgiving" by Isaac Watts, 30
    "Thanksgiving" by F. R. Havergal, 34
    "The Twilight of Thanksgiving" by William D. Kelly, 86
    "We Thank Thee," by Ralph Waldo Emerson, 13

Proclamation, 63
Proclamation by Abraham Lincoln, 40, 65
Proclamation by George Washington, 39, 64

Recipes (see cooking)

Songs
    "Bringing in the Sheaves," 82
    "Count Your Blessings," 14
    "Harvest Hymn," 26
    "We Gather Together," 54
    "We Thank Thee," 81

Stories
    "Captain Christy's Thanksgiving" by Carolyn Sherwin Bailey, 27
    "Davy's Thanksgiving" by J. T. Trowbridge, 20
    "First Harvest-Home in Plymouth" by W. DeLoss Love Jr., 3
    "The First Thanksgiving," 5
    "Helen's Thanksgiving" by Susan Coolidge, 59
    "How Obadiah Brought About Thanksgiving" by Emily Hewitt Leland, 7
    "The Mother of Thanksgiving" by Amy Puetz, 37
    "A Mystery in the Kitchen" by Olive Thorne Miller, 48
    "The Soap Making of Remember Biddle" by Carolyn Sherwin Bailey, 15
    "Squanto" by Mr. Blaisdell and Mr. Ball, 78
    "The Story of Massasoit" by Robert Mackenzie, 32
    "Thankfullest Thanksgiving" by Pauline Shackleford Colyar, 67
    "The Thanksgiving Goose" by Fannie Wilder Brown, 45
    "A Turkey for the Stuffing" by Katherine Grace Hulbert, 83
    "Turning the Thanksgiving Tables" By Carolyn Sherwin Bailey, 73
    "Why He Carried the Turkey" by James Baldwin, 55

Thanksgiving before the Pilgrims, 25

Countdown Books
by Amy Puetz

Countdown to Easter
Memory Making Stories and Activities for 14 Days Leading up to Easter by Amy Puetz
Do you feel that the spiritual significance of Easter has been overshadowed by commercialism? Do you see that Easter candy and the Easter Bunny have become the focus of this holiday? Are you ready to get back to the true meaning of Easter? Get ready to experience the other side of Easter—the one celebrated by people for hundreds of years. *Countdown to Easter* has family friendly stories and activities for every day from the Monday before Palm Sunday to Easter. Imagine your family gathering each day, reading an Easter story, and then participating in a fun activity. This can become a reality with *Countdown to Easter*. The book is divided into daily sections. Each day has a story and an activity that should take about 30 to 45 minutes to complete. The delightful stories in this book were written in the 1800s and early 1900s. The activities include crafts, cooking, riddles, quizzes, hymns, games, and more.

100 pages, paperback, size 8.25x11 inches, black & white illustrations, $17

Countdown to Christmas
Memory Making Stories and Activities for Every Day from December 1st to the 25th by Amy Puetz
Do you long to make this holiday season the best ever? Do you want to slow down this Christmas and enjoy the holiday as they did in times past? If you answered yes to any of these questions, then this wonderful book will brighten your family's Christmas. *Countdown to Christmas* has family friendly stories and activities for every day from December 1st to the 25th. Imagine your family reading a Christmas story each day and then participating in a fun activity together. The book is divided into daily sections. Each day has a story and an activity that will take about 30 to 45 minutes. Most of the stories in this book were written in the 1800s and early 1900s. Some of the language may be old fashioned, but this only adds to the stories' charm! Reading aloud as a family will open up wonderful opportunities for discussions and conversations.

149 pages, paperback, size 8.25x11 inches, black & white illustrations, $19

AVAILABLE AT WWW.AMYPUETZ.COM

Get Ready to Experience History in a Whole New Way!

Touch	Smell	Hear	See	Taste
Crafts, Historical Games, Hands-on Activities	Recipes	Songs, Documents, and Speeches	Classic Art, Videos, and Skits to Perform	Historical Foods

Heroes and Heroines of the Past: American History Curriculum by Amy Puetz

For 1st–6th grades. This is a thirty week history curriculum. Along with the historical information there are exciting stories about historical people. There is a beginner section for 1st and 2nd grades and a more advance section for 3rd through 6th grades. Included in the text are activities that go along with each lesson. Includes three paperback books: Part 1, Part 2, Historical Skits, and three CDs, the Additional Materials CD, Sing Some History Audio CD, and Listen to Some U.S. History MP3 CD. $98.99

Additional Materials CD - This CD has supplemental materials. There are printable timelines, instructions and entertaining videos, color artwork, coloring pages, and much more.

Historical Skits - Performing historical skits is a great way to bring history to life. This book has nineteen skits from the time of Columbus to World War II.

Sing Some History CD - Hear some of the songs that are mentioned in the book. Music is a great way to experience history.

Listen to Some U.S. History MP3 CD - An audio collection of original speeches, poems, sermons, and documents.

Heroes and Heroines of the Past: Coloring Book
This book will keep your students hands busy while they are learning about history. There are pictures to go along with each lesson of the *Heroes and Heroines of the Past: American History*. $9.99

AVAILABLE AT www.AMYPUETZ.COM

www.ingramcontent.com/pod-product-compliance
Lightning Source LLC
Chambersburg PA
CBHW051420070526
44584CB00023B/3512